Success Starts Here
(Things Every Minute Taker Should Know)

Also by Elizabeth J Tucker:

Simply Stress (Stress Management Exercises, Strategies and Techniques)

The 7 Deadly Sins of Chairing Meetings (Let's Get it Right Every Time)

The 5 P's For a Perfect Meeting (A Step-by-step Guide to Navigate Meetings Like a Pro)

Publisher: Shepherd Creative Learning

Success Starts Here
(Things Every Minute Taker Should Know)
By: Elizabeth J Tucker

Publisher's Note:

The author has made every reasonable attempt to achieve complete accuracy of the content in this book prior to going to press. The publisher, the editor and the author cannot accept responsibility for any errors or omissions, however caused.

You should use this information as you see fit, and at your own risk. You should adjust your use of this information and recommendations accordingly.

Finally, use your own wisdom as guidance. Nothing in this Guide is intended to replace common sense, legal, or other professional advice. This book is meant to inform and entertain the reader.

No responsibility for loss or damage occasioned to any person acting, or refraining from action, as a result of the material in this publication can be accepted by the publisher, the author or the editor.

Dedication:

The book is dedicated to Dennis Shepherd (my lovely partner), and Rosemary Tucker and Geoffrey Tucker (my hugely supportive parents).

This book is also dedicated to all the people who have attended our Chairing Successful Meetings and Minute Taking Made Easy training workshops. It's also dedicated to all the chairmen/women and minute takers that I've talked to in the course of my research. Thank you for sharing your views, experiences and questions to help make this book possible.

About the Author:

Elizabeth is based at the edge of the Cotswolds. She has several roles. Elizabeth is a successful author, business consultant, holistic life coach and stress management consultant.

Elizabeth is an innovative presenter with an engaging manner. She has spent many years helping individuals and organisations achieve their goals. Elizabeth writes her books based on her considerable business knowledge and experience.

She describes herself as an enthusiastic go-getter with a passion for helping others reach their full potential or achieve their goals. Elizabeth uses her own unique blend of insight, wisdom and humour in her work. Her catchphrase is "inspiration and support when you need it".

As well as a successful corporate career she has owned and managed several businesses. Since starting her own business in 2003 she has had the privilege of working with a diverse client base. Her clients have included The Chartered Institute of Housing, Blue Chip companies, the British Army, charities, social housing providers, SME and start-up businesses, and personal clients.

Elizabeth is currently working on a project to create a series of self-help business books. These will be available as paperbacks and Kindle books. You can find out when these are published by viewing her LinkedIn profile (liz-tucker/10/531/68/) or following her on Twitter (@liztucker03).

Table of Contents

Preface

In the course of my research I was staggered by how little training and support minute takers receive. Organisations often provide their staff with access to training for all sorts of skills development. However, minute taking doesn't commonly appear on the radar.

I have been fortunate enough to receive formal training for all aspects of meetings. However, the good news is you don't need to attend a training course to be a good minute taker.

I've been involved with meetings for most of my adult life. My experience has included being an attendee, chairperson and minute taker. I've been involved in formal, business and informal meetings, so I know a thing or two about meetings.

My expertise and the lack of support many minute takers receive prompted me to write Success Starts Here (Things Every Minute Taker Should Know). Success Starts Here is a practical guide that will help new and experienced minute takers. It's designed to be your 'go-to' book when you need a little help.

Although minute taking requires a specific set of skills, anyone can learn effective minute taking skills. By the end of this book you will know how to create clear, concise and accurate minutes. Then all you need is plenty of regular practice to hone your new skills.

When I decided to write this book it occurred to me that successful meetings involve more than just a good set of minutes. This prompted me to write a trilogy of books covering the broad topic of meetings and minute taking.

Success Starts Here (Things Every Minute Taker Should Know) covers the meeting secretary's role and the minute taker's role. This book encompasses agenda styles and minutes as these documents are closely linked. The other two books in this series are:

1. The 7 Deadly Sins of Chairing Meetings (Let's Get it Right Every Time)

2. The 5 P's For a Perfect Meeting (A Step-by-step Guide to Navigate Meetings Like a Pro)

Each book is designed to be a practical guide. You will find handy hints and exercises throughout each book. The exercises will test your knowledge or provide you with an opportunity to think about how you and your organisation currently operate.

I wrote Success Starts Here to remove some of your fears about minute taking. I hope by the time you reach the end of the book I will have succeeded. Minute taking is a very useful and transferrable skill. There are always opportunities for good minute takers so you never need to be short of work. Good luck!

1. Introduction

Although most attendees don't have the skills to be an effective minute taker they are very critical of poor minutes. Everyone has an opinion about what good minutes look like. By understanding the rules of minute taking you will be in a position to be the subject matter expert.

By the end of this book you will be able to:

1. Understand the meeting secretary's role and the minute taker's role

2. Understand the different styles of agenda and select the right one for your meetings

3. Present a professional looking agenda that follows protocol

4. Feel more confident about note taking during meetings

5. Understand the different styles of minutes and what should be included

6. Create clear, concise and accurate minutes

7. Know when to issue the agenda and the minutes

8. Create the right style of agenda and minutes for your meetings

Exercise: Quick Minute Taking Quiz

How much do you already know about minutes and minute taking? Take this quick quiz to test your knowledge. Each question is multiple choice so all you need to do is pick the correct answer:

1. How many styles of minutes are there? - One/Three/Ten

2. Minutes are just minutes. The same style of minutes is suitable for every meeting - Yes/No

3. After the minutes are issued everyone should read them and let the minute taker know if there are any errors. The minutes can then be amended before the next meeting - Yes/No

4. Anyone who wants a copy of the minutes can have them? - Yes/No

5. The minute taker owns the minutes as he/she created them, and they are the minute taker's personal notes - Yes/No

6. The minute taker is one of the attendees and so is expected to participate in the discussions - Yes/No

7. The minutes should be issued with the agenda for the next meeting - Yes/No

You will find the answers to these questions in the Appendices section at the end of the book.

Meetings are vital for effective leadership, business management and good communication. However, when was the last time you heard someone say 'that was a really good meeting'?

Meetings save time, and increase staff motivation and productivity. They can be useful for problem solving, and are great for creating new ideas and initiatives. Most importantly, meetings prevent 'not invented here' syndrome and diffuse conflict in a way that emails cannot.

A meeting without minutes is nothing more than a get-together. It cannot be deemed a good use of company time and money as no one will be accountable for the actions. In short, if a meeting is necessary then so are minutes.

It's a common myth that 'anyone can take minutes without any training. In truth, minute taking is a skill that can be learnt by anyone, but like every other skill it takes practice. Very few people have a natural gift for minute taking.

Another myth that needs to be dispelled is shorthand secretaries automatically make good minute takers. These are two very different roles and require different skills. In fact shorthand secretaries often struggle with minute taking, although some can fulfil both roles.

A shorthand secretary is used to capturing everything that is said. A good minute taker records what was discussed, not what was said. There's a subtle difference between the two. Minute taking is about summarising what was discussed, not capturing everything.

Success Starts Here (Things Every Minute Taker Should Know) is a practical guide. It will take you through each stage of the meeting secretary's and minute taker's role. Purchasing this book is a small investment that will pay dividends by increasing your personal toolkit.

Exercise: My Experience of Minute Taking

Minute taking is a role that most people dread. Very few people ever admit to enjoying the task of minute taking, which is a shame as it's not as difficult as you might imagine. There are no right or wrong answers to this exercise.

Instructions:

Spend a few minutes reflecting on your first meeting as a minute taker.

1. Overall how did you find your first experience of minute taking? Did you enjoy it or was it terrifying? Did the chairperson provide all the support you needed during and after the meeting?

2. Did you find minute taking easy or challenging?

3. What did you learn from the experience?

4. Did you come away from the meeting feeling that you had acquired some useful new skills?

5. What did you do differently at future meetings as a result of this one?

6. Do you believe your minute taking skills have improved since that first experience?

The minute takers role is a responsible one, but is rarely given the respect it deserves. The role is often allocated to someone who has received no formal training. Furthermore, minute takers often receive little or no support during meetings. Added to that, the minute taker often gets involved in some or all of the discussions.

The end result is a stressed minute taker and poor quality minutes. No wonder most people dislike minute taking. It doesn't need to be like this.

With training or clear instructions and practice anyone can take good quality minutes. However, few people have a natural gift for minute taking.

The key skills of a good minute taker are:

1. The ability to listen with an open mind

2. Able to capture key information in note form

3. They know what to capture and what to ignore

4. They record the actions, action owner and date for the actions to be completed

5. He/she has the confidence to stop the meeting if he/she doesn't understand the discussion

6. They have good assertiveness skills. Good minute takers are comfortable stopping the meeting if an action completion date hasn't been agreed

14

7. They are able to produce clear, concise and accurate minutes in a timely manner

8. They are able to write in plain English

Unfortunately, there is no substitute for practice. However, this book provides lots of useful hints and tips to help remove the fear factor. Getting rid of the fear factor will make the task of minute taking less daunting.

2. Frequently Asked Questions

In the course of my research I have spoken to many minute takers. Their feedback has been invaluable in helping with creating a book that answers the most common questions.

There seems to be a common thread of difficulties experienced by minute takers. This chapter deals with the difficulties minute takers have talked to me about. Here you will find details of the most common issues and my suggestions for resolving them:

Question/Issue: I'm not sure how to prepare the agenda. I don't know what order to list things
Answer: The good news is all agendas should follow the same order. The order is - Apologies, Welcome, Minutes of the previous meeting, Matters arising, Reports, Main agenda items, Any other business, and Date of the next meeting

Question/Issue: I don't know what I'm responsible for as the minute taker
Answer: It depends whether you are just the minute taker or the minute taker and meeting secretary. The meeting secretary is responsible for preparing and issuing the agenda, getting the updates and booking the venue etc. The minute taker is responsible for note taking during the meeting and then creating and issuing the minutes

Question/Issue: I'm new to the organisation and I don't have much knowledge of the meeting I'm taking the minutes for
Answer: If possible try to attend your first meeting as an observer. If this isn't possible ask the chairperson to brief you. This briefing should include the group dynamics, purpose of the meeting, technical references, and what the chairperson expects from you. If you need help and support don't be scared to ask for it

Question/Issue: Our chairperson never introduces people at the start of the meeting. This means sometimes I don't know who the action owners are
Answer: Perhaps your chairperson doesn't realise that it's good practice to make sure everyone knows each other. A gentle word might help. Arrive early for each meeting and introduce yourself to the people you don't already know. This will save time during the meeting as you won't have to keep stopping to ask people's names

Question/Issue: I always end up being tucked away in a corner. I can't easily see who is talking or make eye contact with the chairperson
Answer: Make sure you arrive early and position yourself where you find it most helpful to sit. If everyone is already seated when you arrive politely ask someone to move

Question/Issue: Some people talk too fast in the meeting, which means I struggle to keep up
Answer: Ask the chairperson to summarise what he/she wants you to capture for the minutes

Question/Issue: In some of our meetings more than one person talks at the same time. This makes it very difficult to follow the discussion
Answer: Speak up! Tell the group that you cannot take good quality notes if more than one person talks at once

Question/Issue: The discussion jumps from one item to another before any of them are finished
Answer: Your chairperson is clearly not in control of his/her meeting. In the first instance speak to the chairperson. If things don't improve you will have to point this out to the entire group

Question/Issue: I've noticed that some people keep repeating themselves at our meetings
Answer: It's the chairperson's responsibility to deal with this. In terms of note taking, simply ignore anything that has already been captured for the minutes

Question/Issue: There is a personal feud going on between two of my colleagues. This often spills over into the meeting
Answer: It's the chairperson's responsibility to deal with this. If he/she is oblivious or chooses to ignore it, explain the impact it's having on your note taking during the meeting

Question/Issue: We don't stick to the agenda as our chairperson allows the meeting to drift onto other matters
Answer: Speak to the chairperson. Meetings that become a talking shop rarely achieve their objectives

Question/Issue: I can't understand my own handwriting/notes after the meeting
Answer: You are probably trying to take too many notes during the meeting and so rushing to keep up. Slow down, take fewer notes, write in bullet points and don't worry about the punctuation or grammar

Question/Issue: Some of our meetings involve long, confusing discussions and I don't know which bits are important
Answer: Don't sit there struggling. Ask your chairperson to clarify what needs minuting

Question/Issue: I don't know what to capture when an argument breaks out
Answer: Treat this like any other discussion in the meeting. Make a note of the discussion, not details of the argument. Also, ask the chairperson what he/she wants you to minute. The chairperson may decide none of the discussion should be minuted

Question/Issue: I regularly seem to miss a relevant point in the meeting
Answer: Until you feel confident, why not ask someone else to take a set of notes too. After the meeting you can compare notes. As your confidence grows you will need less help

Question/Issue: Although I'm the minute taker I sometimes get involved in the discussion and struggle to take good quality notes at the same time
Answer: Ask someone else to take notes for any agenda item where you are an active participant. The minute taker shouldn't be expected to contribute to the discussion

Question/Issue: Sometimes we have too many agenda items. Should we finish the meeting on time and ignore what hasn't been dealt with, or should we stay and finish the meeting?
Answer: Always finish on time. Any agenda items not dealt with should be carried forward to the next meeting. The minutes need to reflect this. The agenda is either being overloaded or your chairperson has poor time management skills

Question/Issue: I don't know how to present the minutes so they look professional
Answer: Start by ensuring the header and numbering matches on the agenda and minutes. As a bare minimum your minutes need to include the action, action owner and completion date. Most minutes also include a brief summary of the discussion too

Question/Issue: I'm not sure who is entitled to a copy of the minutes. I don't want to issue the minutes to people who aren't entitled to a copy
Answer: Everyone who was invited to the meeting is entitled to a copy of the minutes; whether they were present or not. It's the chairperson's responsibility to decide who else is entitled to a copy of the minutes. If anyone asks for a copy direct them to the chairperson

Question/Issue: The chairperson doesn't approve the minutes until a few days before the next meeting. What should I do?

Answer: Ideally the chairperson should approve the minutes soon after the minutes are produced so you can issue them. If this doesn't happen it's better to issue the minutes on time. You will have chance to change the minutes at the next meeting if they are factually incorrect

Question/Issue: I'm new to minute taking and I'm just nervous about getting it right

Answer: This is perfectly normal. Practice makes perfect. In the meantime there is sufficient detail in this book to enable you to create good quality minutes

Question/Issue: Should I used justified margins for my minutes, or a justified left margin and a ragged right margin

Answer: This is a matter of personal choice. During our research we discovered that people were equally split on the use of justified margins. You might like to check to see if your organisation has a preferred style

3. Types of Meeting

Although this book is about the agenda and minutes, it's important to understand the different types of meeting. This may influence the style of agenda and minutes required for the meeting.

Meetings fall into three categories. These are formal meetings, business meetings and informal meetings.

3.1 Formal Meetings

There are lots of different types of formal meeting. I have provided a summary of the most common formal meetings for your information.

Annual General Meeting (AGM)
As the name suggests, this is an annual meeting. It's often a mandatory meeting, comprising the company's directors and shareholders.

This type of meeting generally uses a full agenda although some organisations may opt for the objectives agenda. Before creating the agenda, check with the chairperson to identify which he/she prefers.

Extraordinary General Meeting (EGM)
An EGM can be called at any time between AGMs if shareholder approval is required. The same rules apply to the meeting as apply to AGMs.

This type of meeting generally uses a full agenda although some organisations may opt for the objectives agenda. Before creating the agenda, check with the chairperson to identify which he/she prefers.

Board Meetings
A board meeting is attended by the board of a company, usually directors. These are often regular meetings, and the purpose is to discuss company business.

Generally the full agenda is used for board meetings. The basic or objectives agenda could be used if the chairperson prefers either of these options. Ask the chairperson to confirm which style of agenda they prefer.

A Standing Committee
A standing committee is a sub-committee of the company's board. This committee has delegated tasks, and meets regularly to discuss these.
A full or basic agenda is usually used for this type of meeting.

One-off Committee
This committee is set up by the board to look at a single issue. The committee can meet as frequently or infrequently as they choose.

Generally a basic agenda is suitable for this type of meeting. Having said that it's for the chairperson to select the style of agenda he/she prefers.

Public Meetings
As the name suggests, public meetings are open to anyone. Local government and private action groups often use this type of meeting.

A full or basic agenda is suitable for this type of meeting. Find out which the chairperson prefers.

Conference
Most conferences are private affairs but some are open to the public. Conferences generally involve several presentations, which are introduced by the chairperson.

A basic agenda is generally used for this type of meeting. Someone will be expected to minute any actions. Copies of the presentations should be attached to the minutes for a historical record.

External Meetings
External meetings involve people from your own organisation along with representatives from outside the organisation.

It's a matter of personal choice or company policy regarding the style of agenda to be used. The full or basic agenda is suitable for this type of meeting. It's rare for the objectives agenda to be selected for external meetings.

3.2 Business Meetings

Business meetings are sometimes known as workplace meetings. These are the most common type of meeting that most people attend. Business meetings are vital for effective leadership, business management and good communication throughout the organisation.

Although business meetings generally involve a group of people you could have a one-to-one business meeting. Due to the nature of performance appraisals, a business meeting is ideal. It will provide the structure needed for this type of meeting.

The basic agenda is suitable for business meetings. Some organisations prefer to use a full agenda, but it's very rare for the objectives agenda to be used for business meetings. Expect to create minutes for all business meetings.

3.3 Informal Meetings

Just like formal meetings, informal meetings come in many guises. Informal meetings should never take place around someone's desk. Psychologically this makes it easier to end the meeting and walk away. Research shows that meetings around someone's desk tend to go on longer than necessary.

A basic agenda is ideal for all informal meetings. If you decide not to create an agenda for informal meetings then at least create a list of topics for discussion. A meeting without and agenda or list of topics is likely to end up as nothing more than a talking shop.

Impromptu Meetings
This style of meeting can be very helpful for reaching decisions quickly. This is an ideal meeting for small groups that have an issue that needs a speedy resolution. Ideally you don't want a group size of more than four people for impromptu meetings.

Ideas Sharing Meetings
Some like to call these 'ideas sharing' meetings. Others prefer to refer to them as 'brainstorming' or 'thought showers'. Whatever you call it, they all amount to the same thing - a very short meeting for generating ideas. For maximum impact these meetings should be no longer than 30-40 minutes.

Even though the meeting is informal, minutes are helpful. Minutes make attendees accountable and ensure actions are completed.

4. Roles and Responsibilities

There are two roles. These are the meeting secretary and the minute taker. Everything that happens up to the pre-meeting is the responsibility of the meeting secretary. Everything that happens during and after the meeting is the responsibility of the minute taker. In reality, often the same person takes on both roles unless the chairperson prefers to plan their own meetings.

Some chairmen/women don't bother with a briefing session with the minute taker. This is either because they don't know about this briefing or don't value it. A chairperson/minute taker briefing is worth the effort as it helps improve the efficiency of meetings.

I have separated the roles of meeting secretary and minute taker. I have documented the responsibilities for each so you know what is expected of you regardless of which role you do.

4.1 The Meeting Secretary

How much or how little the meeting secretary does is down to each individual chairman/woman. Some chairmen/women like to delegate the entire meeting planning phase, while others like to do it themselves. Find out how your chairman/woman likes to work.

For the purpose of this book I have assumed the meeting secretary is going to be very involved in the planning phase. If you are expected to plan the meeting here are the tasks you may be asked to do:

1. Book the meeting room and refreshments etc

2. Book parking spaces for external attendees, if required

3. Invite the attendees (unless the chairperson has already done this, or they already know they are expected to attend)

4. When inviting the attendees make sure they know why they have been invited, and what is expected of them. It's the chairperson's responsibility to do this. He/she may delegate this task to you

5. If your meeting has visitors it's important to ensure they too know what is expected of them. Advise visitors if they are required for the entire meeting or not. If not, confirm what time they are expected to arrive

6. Find out which style of agenda is required for the meeting. The Basic Agenda is suitable for most business meetings

7. Canvass agenda items. For monthly or less frequent meetings the cut-off date is eight working days before the meeting. For weekly meetings the cut-off date is four working days before the meeting

8. The cut-off date relates to reports and any other documents as well as agenda items

9. Prepare the agenda and seek the chairperson's approval before issuing it. If the chairperson doesn't approve the agenda you will have to issue it without approval

10. The meeting secretary is expected to verify that all outstanding actions have been completed. If not, get an update on what has been done and what is outstanding. Share this information with the chairperson and minute taker before the meeting date

11. Issue the agenda to everyone who is invited to the meeting. For monthly meetings issue the agenda at least five working days before the meeting. For weekly meetings issue the agenda at least three working days before the meeting. It's important that everyone has time to prepare for the meeting

12. Prepare the chairperson's agenda. This is a more detailed copy of the agenda issued to everyone else

If your role is just meeting secretary then your task is complete. From now on the minute taker is responsible for the remaining actions.

Handy hint: Do not get into the habit of accepting late agenda items as you will need to keep re-issuing the agenda. This is time consuming and a waste of time.

4.2 The Minute Taker

Your primary role is note taking during the meeting and converting these into clear, concise and accurate minutes. However, you will have some tasks before the meeting.

1. Once the agenda and other documents have been issued print copies for the meeting. As the minute taker you will need your own personal copy of the agenda, minutes of the previous meeting, and any other documents that have been issued to the attendees.

If the chairperson is going to sign the minutes you will need to print a copy for signing. Print a small number or spare copies of each document for those people who forget their copy

2. Read the agenda and make sure you understand each agenda item. This will help you during the meeting

3. Ensure you have updates for all the actions from the previous meeting. The meeting secretary will have obtained these for you. If you have this information ahead of the meeting you won't need to write it down during the meeting

4. The day before the meeting have a short briefing session with the chairperson

5. Prepare your notepad ahead of the meeting. This saves time when the meeting starts and makes the task of note taking much easier

6. Arrive at least 15 minutes before the start of the meeting. This will give you chance to check the room is laid out correctly and check teas, coffees, equipment etc. It's also an opportunity for you and the chairperson to agree where you're both going to sit

7. If possible make a note of the attendees as soon as they arrive. This will save time during the meeting

8. As soon as the meeting starts make a note of any attendees not already recorded. Create a list of initials of each attendee. This will save time during the meeting. It takes too long to write people's names in full during the meeting

8. During the meeting take as many notes as you feel necessary. As you gain experience and confidence you will write fewer notes. Make sure all the actions are properly recorded as you probably won't remember all the details after the meeting

9. Create a set of draft minutes as soon as possible after the meeting. If possible do this straightaway; certainly not later than two working days after the meeting (monthly or less frequent meetings).

In the case of weekly meetings you will need to do this one working day after the meeting

10. Email the draft minutes to the chairperson for review and approval. Note: this is not an opportunity for the chairperson to change the minutes unless they are factually incorrect

11. Issue the minutes as soon as possible after the meeting. The sooner they are issued the greater the chance of people reading them. For monthly or less frequent meetings the minutes should be issued not later than five working days after the meeting.

In the case of weekly meetings the minutes must be issued not later than two working days after the meeting

Handy hint: Although you will often be asked to amend the minutes once they have been issued, the answer is no. The minutes should not be altered until the next meeting. People will need to keep their comments until the meeting.

Exercise: Review the Meeting Secretary/Minute Taker's Role

Before moving forward this is a good opportunity to review your current role as the meeting secretary or minute taker.

Instructions:

Consider the following questions:

1. Are you currently the meeting secretary, minute taker, or responsible for both roles?

2. Do you currently do each of the tasks identified for these roles? If not, what aren't you currently doing?

3. Do you adhere to the good practice timescales?

4. Is there anything you've learnt about the meeting secretary's role or minute taker's role?

5. Is there anything you can do differently to increase your efficiency in either of these roles?

5. Planning the Meeting

There are various activities involved with planning a meeting. It's not simply a matter of creating an agenda and turning up at the meeting.

It's the chairperson who decides a meeting is necessary. He/she is also ultimately responsible for inviting attendees and making sure everyone knows what is expected of them. Chairmen/women often choose to delegate this task to the meeting secretary.

The meeting secretary may also be involved in booking the meeting room, refreshments, parking spaces etc.

Before you can plan the agenda you need to understand the aim and expected outcomes of the meeting. By understanding the objectives of the meeting you will be able to ensure each agenda item is relevant.

The meeting secretary is also responsible for obtaining updates regarding all the actions from the previous meeting. Collate this information and share it with the chairperson and minute taker before the next meeting. This makes the minute taker's job easier during the meeting.

Preparing for the meeting can be time-consuming, especially if you have to chase the group for their agenda items. A good meeting secretary has excellent time management skills. You will be expected to fit this task in around your normal role in the organisation.

It's important to find out what the chairperson intends to do, and what he/she is expecting you to do. This will prevent duplication of effort.

5.1 What is an Agenda?

An agenda is a list or plan of the matters for discussion at the meeting. However it looks the agenda is an essential part of formal and business meetings. It's useful for informal meetings, although you could simply create a list of matters to be discussed.

In case you doubt that an agenda is necessary, here are some reasons for having an agenda:

1. To ensure the meeting is an efficient use of company time and money

2. To ensure everyone knows what will be discussed at the meeting

3. To ensure everything important is dealt with during the meeting

4. To make sure only relevant topics are covered

5. It makes chairing the meeting easier

6. It makes the minute taker's role easier as he/she has headings for the notes

7. It gives structure to the meeting

In short, never plan a business meeting without an agenda. If you don't want an agenda for informal meetings, at least make sure you have a list of topics for discussion.

There are no two ways about it, poor planning and preparation leads to an unsatisfactory meeting. The time spent compiling the agenda will help ensure an efficient meeting. It will make the task of minute taking easier and may help reduce the meeting time. It provides the chairperson and minute taker with a structure to work with. In short, it's worth the effort.

Spending time creating the right agenda will ensure that never again do you have irrelevant agenda items as part of your meeting. Little steps like this will make a big difference to the overall effectiveness of meetings.

5.2 Obtaining Agenda Items

Always give a deadline for the receipt of agenda items and stick to it. Discourage late submissions by not accepting late agenda items, apart from in exceptional circumstances. Any agenda item that arrives after the cut-off date should be held back until the next meeting.

If the meeting is monthly or less frequent the cut-off date for agenda items is 8 working days before the meeting. For weekly meetings the cut-off date is 4 working days before the meeting.

Each contributor should advise how much meeting time is required for their agenda item. The meeting secretary needs to know how long each agenda item requires. This is essential for efficient scheduling. You or the chairperson could decide to allow less time than requested if you have a full agenda.

Don't feel you must include agenda items just because you have been asked to. The following are reasons **not** to include an agenda item:

1. The item isn't relevant to the meeting

2. It doesn't involve the majority of the attendees

3. It could be dealt with outside the meeting

4. There are too many agenda items and this is one of the least important

If in doubt ask the chairperson whether he/she wishes to include the agenda item or not.

If you decide to accept late agenda items they should be treated as 'Any other business'. Otherwise it will be necessary to reissue the agenda. It's a waste of your time to keep reissuing the agenda

Handy hint: Spend time getting the agenda right. This means you won't have to waste time rewriting and reissuing it.

5.3 Agenda Styles

There are three styles of agenda. These are basic agenda, full agenda and objectives agenda. Treat the agenda is like any other business document. Regardless of the style of agenda you choose, it should be written in black and white and your normal business font. Arial or Verdana are the preferred business fonts for most organisations. This is not the time to produce a creative work of art.

There are pros and cons associated with each style of agenda. I have provided details of each agenda style so you can choose the right one for your meetings.

Basic Agenda
The basic agenda is the most commonly used style of agenda for business meetings. It's suitable for most business meetings.

For anyone new to creating agendas this style of agenda is ideal. It's easy to create, and most meeting secretaries can do this with little or no input form the chairperson. It's a good starting point for anyone new to creating agendas.

There is a downside to the basic agenda. The headings can sometimes be vague. This can lead to misunderstanding about what is going to be discussed under each heading. If you choose the basic agenda ensure the headings are clear and specific.

If you use the basic agenda for your meetings the chairperson needs to be strong and disciplined. Otherwise attendees may use the generic headings to discuss a variety of topics, some of which are irrelevant to the meeting.

Basic agendas are ideal for meetings where everyone understands the required outcomes. This style of agenda is also popular for report-back and project planning meetings.

Apart from 'Apologies' each item on the basic agenda is given an agenda item number.

The length of the agenda will depend on the number of main agenda items you have to discuss.

Full Agenda
The full agenda is often used for formal meetings (e.g. board meetings, AGM's etc). The full agenda provides more detailed information than the basic agenda. It contains subheadings where there is more than one discussion point under a particular agenda item.

Although it's great for the attendees, the meeting secretary often requires help to create this style of agenda. You should be aware it takes longer to create this style of agenda.

'Apologies' is the only agenda item that isn't numbered.

The length of the agenda will depend on the number of main agenda items you have to discuss.

Objectives Agenda
The layout of the objectives agenda appears similar to the full agenda. The primary difference between these two styles of agenda is the terminology used. The objectives agenda is not commonly used these days as it's very wordy and makes meetings even longer.

The objectives agenda provides clear guidance on what has to be achieved rather than what is to be discussed. If you choose to use an objectives agenda, here is a list of common phrases:

To receive...
To decide...
To discuss...
To agree...
To approve...
To establish...
To explore...
To select...
To review...
To confirm...

5.4 Agenda Layout

Regardless of which style of agenda you opt for every agenda should have a clear header that contains the following information:

Name of the group that is meeting

Date and start time of the meeting

Venue (full meeting address)

You can centre or left justify the header section of your agenda. This is a matter of personal choice. If it's any help, most organisations opt to centre the header section and left justify the rest of the document. I have left justified the header section in the examples I've created.

Leave at least two blank lines after the header section. The white space helps to make the document visually appealing and easy to read.

The heading 'Agenda' is generally centred. Leave at least two blank lines after the heading. Once again, this is to make the document easy to read.

Moving onto the main body of the document... decide whether you are going to use the basic, full or objectives agenda style. Whichever you choose, the same layout and numbering must be used for the agenda and the minutes.

Ideally, you should be aiming to get the entire agenda on a single A4 page. This isn't always possible for lengthy meetings with lots of matters to discuss. The length of your agenda will dictate the line spacing you use to separate the agenda items.

The order of agenda items is the same for each of the agenda styles. Present your agenda in the following order:

Apologies

Welcome, introductions and administration

Minutes of the previous meeting

Matters arising

Reports

Main agenda items

Any other business

Date of next meeting

All of this information forms part of the audit trail. An internal quality auditor should be able to easily match the two documents up during an audit inspection.

Currently the most popular fonts for business writing are Arial or Verdana. These are both clear, easy to read fonts, which makes them a popular choice. By varying the font size for different parts of the document you make it easier for the reader to spot what they are looking for. Here are my suggestions for your agenda document:

Name of the group or meeting - Arial 14 or 16 point bold text

Date and start time of the meeting - Arial 12 point bold text

Meeting venue - Arial 12 point bold text

Document title - Agenda - Arial 14 or 16 point bold text

Main headings - Arial 12 point bold text

Sub-headings (full and objectives agenda) - Arial 11 point bold text

Objectives description - Arial 11 point text (objectives agenda only)

5.5 Agenda Examples

I thought you might find it helpful to have an example of a basic agenda, full agenda and objectives agenda.

Example of a Basic Agenda
Here is an example of the layout of a basic agenda.

Name of the group that is meeting
Date and start time of the meeting
Venue (full meeting address)

Agenda

Apologies

1. Welcome, introductions and administration

2. Minutes of the previous meeting

3. Matters arising
Maternity cover for Sukhi Patel (PC) 5.0
Replacement scheme manager for Redrock Place (SP) 6.0
Resolve anti-social behaviour issues with the tenant at 10 Parsons Lane (BE) 7.0

4. Reports
Finance Report (FF)
Company Risk Assessment (RP)

5. Official opening of the Sun Rising Village Development by Barrie Boulder MP

6. Training budget and plans for the current financial year

7. Purchase of additional land at Sun Rising Village (HH)

8. Any other business

9. Date of next meeting

Example of a Full Agenda

As you will see from the example below, the full agenda is far more detailed than the basic agenda. It's important to include sub-headings for each discussion point.

Name of the group that is meeting
Date and start time of the meeting
Venue (full meeting address)

Agenda

Apologies

1. Welcome, introductions and administration (or a variation on this)

2. Minutes of the previous meeting

3. Matters arising
3.1 Maternity cover for Sukhi Patel (PC) 5.0
3.2 Replacement scheme manager for Redrock Place (SP) 6.3
3.3 Resolve anti-social behaviour issues with the tenant at 10 Parsons Lane (BE) 7.3

4. Reports
4.1 Finance Report (FF)
4.2 Company Risk Assessment (RP)

5. Official opening of the Sun Rising Village Development by Barrie Boulder MP
5.1 Timetable for visit (draft timetable attached) (WW)
5.2 Duties Barrie Boulder will perform (RC)
5.3 Publicity for the event (SS)
5.4 Security issues (TT)

6. Training budget and plans for the current financial year
6.1 Training budget (FF)
6.2 Agree essential training programmes
6.3 Mentors for graduate trainees
7. Purchase of additional land at Sun Rising Village (HH)
7.1 The likely cost of purchasing the land
7.2 The number and style of properties to be built
7.3 Financing the project (FF)
7.4 Timescale for completing the project

8. Any other business

9. Date of next meeting

Example of an Objectives Agenda
The objectives agenda isn't commonly used as it's wordy and cumbersome. Here is an example in case you want to create an objectives agenda for your meeting.

Name of the group that is meeting
Date and start time of the meeting
Venue (full meeting address)

Agenda

Apologies

1. Welcome, introductions and administration (or a variation on this)
To welcome everyone to the meeting, make the introductions and deal with housekeeping matters

2. Minutes of the previous meeting
To review and adopt the minutes of the previous meeting

3. Matters arising
3.1 To provide an update on the maternity cover for Sukhi Patel (PC) 5.0
3.2 To appoint a replacement scheme manager for Redrock Place (SP) 6.3
3.3 To provide an update on the anti-social behaviour issues with the tenant at 10 Parsons Lane (BE) 7.3

4. Reports
4.1 To receive the finance report from FF

4.2 To receive the group's updated risk assessment from RC

4.3 To receive the training budget and plans for the current financial year report from MM

5. Official opening of the Sun Rising Village Development by Barrie Boulder MP
5.1 To finalise the timetable for visit (draft timetable attached) (WW)

5.2 To discuss the duties Barrie Boulder will perform (RC)

5.3 To agree the publicity for the event (SS)

5.4 To discuss the security issues (TT)

6. Training budget and plans for the current financial year
6.1 To agree the training budget (FF)

6.2 To agree what is essential training for the current financial year

6.3 To select the mentors for this year's intake of graduate trainees

7. Purchase of additional land at Sun Rising Village (HH)
7.1 To discuss the likely cost of purchasing the land and agree if this is financially viable

7.2 To agree the number and style of properties to be built

7.3 To agree how the project should be financed (FF)

7.4 To discuss the timescale for completing the project

8. Any other business
To discuss any urgent items presented under 'Any other business'

9. Date of next meeting
To agree the date for the next meeting

5.6 Agenda Headings Explained

Apologies
This heading appears at the top of the agenda but is not given an agenda item number. 'Apologies' is just listed as a reminder for attendees to send their apologies if they know they won't be attending.

Handy hint: Apologies are not numbered on the agenda because they aren't numbered in the minutes. It's important that the numbering matches on both documents.

Welcome, Introductions and Administration
As you might expect this is when the chairperson opens the meeting, and deals with all the housekeeping matters. It's a chance for the chairperson to confirm the aim and objectives of the meeting.

This is also the point when the chairperson asks for apologies and identifies anyone who is absent (but was expected). It's important to capture this information for the minutes.

Minutes of the Previous Meeting
The chairperson will use this item to invite the group to adopt the minutes of the previous meeting. If this is the group's first meeting there won't be any minutes to approve. In which case, this item wouldn't appear on the agenda.

If there were any inaccuracies in the minutes, they should be flagged up during this agenda item. This will be the only opportunity to amend the minutes once they've been drafted and issued.

Matters Arising
These are all the actions from the previous meeting. Each action should be listed along with the action owner and reference number from the previous minutes. This is so the chairperson knows who to ask for an update regarding the action.

Some organisations like to have a table of actions as well as this heading on the agenda. If so, the table of actions will be a separate document that is usually only given to the chairperson and minute taker.

Reports
Anything under this heading on the agenda is not for discussion. The chairperson will only invite queries relating to any of the reports. If a report is going to be discussed in detail it will appear under the main agenda items, not the reports heading.

Next to the name of the report, write the name or initials of the report owner. For example, Finance Report (Freddy Fiscal). Always include the report owner's initials in case of queries regarding the report.

Main Agenda Items
These should be listed in order or importance or the order the chairperson wants to discuss them. This will ensure the most important topics are discussed, even if the meeting runs outs of time.

Each topic for discussion should be given its own agenda item number and heading.

Handy hint: Don't start with a contentious or sensitive matter. People relax more as the meeting progresses, so sandwich contentious or sensitive matters between less evocative topics.

Any Other Business

At the time of producing the agenda, this will be a heading without anything to discuss.

Date of Next Meeting

This agenda item is either to fix the date of the next meeting or remind everyone of the date already agreed.

5.7 Other Things to Consider

Here are some other things to consider when planning the agenda. If someone is going to lead the discussion for a particular agenda item include their name or initials next to the agenda item. For example: **5. Purchase of land at Sun Rising Village** (HH and FF)

If there are any reports or other documents that will form part of the meeting, these should be issued with the agenda. There isn't time during meetings to read documents and then have a meaningful discussion.

If you are issuing documents with the agenda, write the agenda item number on the front of the relevant document/report. This cross-referencing helps the attendees before and during the meeting.

Never be tempted to overload the agenda as you will just end up with matters that don't get discussed. This creates unnecessary extra work.

If an item doesn't get discussed a note will need to be added to the minutes. Typically the note will state [agenda item and title] wasn't discussed due to lack of time. You will be expected to schedule these agenda items for the next meeting.

If you have too many agenda items for the time available ask the chairperson which ones he/she wants to include. If any items aren't included on the agenda, notify the requester before the agenda is issued. No one likes to discover their agenda item has been dropped by reading the agenda.

Handy hint: If you have to drop someone's agenda item offer them a priority listing for the next meeting.

Exercise: Preparing the Agenda

Most often the task of creating the agenda is delegated to the meeting secretary. This is fine as long as you have some guidelines from the chairperson.

Instructions:

Consider the following questions about your experience of creating an agenda.

1. What guidance or instructions do you receive from your chairperson before you create the agenda?

2. Is every agenda item always accepted, or do you consider its relevance to the overall meeting?

3. How do you decide how much time is required/permitted for each agenda item?

4. Do you advise attendees if their agenda item isn't going to be included?

5. How much support do you receive from the chairperson when you're creating the agenda?

6. Does the chairperson always review the agenda before it's issued?

7. Thinking about your current process for creating the agenda, how can you improve this?

5.8 The Chairperson's Agenda

This is sometimes referred to as the chairperson's brief. The chairperson's copy of the agenda is more detailed than the one issued to other attendees.

The chairperson's agenda includes timings and details of the desired outcome for each agenda item. It also contains any background information that might be helpful to the chairperson during the meeting.

Here are some typical outcomes that often appear the on the chairperson's copy of the agenda.

1. Decision required

2. Discussion only

3. Share information with the group

4. Planning. This may involve a workshop session or agreeing plans for a project

5. An ideas generating discussion only

6. Obtain feedback regarding an action, event or outcome

7. Find solution to a problem

8. Agree targets, budgets, aims etc

9. A policy statement to be shared with the group

10. Team building or motivation

11. Guest speaker. Note: guest speakers are usually there to discuss something that doesn't normally feature as part of the meeting

Timings on the chairperson's copy of the agenda are essential to ensure all matters are concluded in the time available. Include the start time of each main agenda item, not the sub-headings.

Handy hint: Add the timings when creating the agenda, not afterwards. This will enable you to see what can realistically be achieved in the time available.

5.9 Issuing the Agenda

Whether the chairperson has been involved in creating the agenda or not he/she should review the agenda before it's issued. This is the chairperson's opportunity to amend or remove agenda items.

For monthly or less frequent meetings the agenda should be issued at least four working days before the meeting. For weekly meetings the agenda should be issued at least three working days before the meeting.

It's fine to issue the agenda early, but it's bad practice to issue the agenda late. Issuing the agenda in a timely manner is essential to give everyone an opportunity to prepare for the meeting.

Once the agenda has been issued don't amend it and reissue it unless this is unavoidable. If there are any urgent agenda items these can be dealt with under 'Any other business'. The chairperson needs to grant permission for items to be included under 'Any other business'. Update the chairperson's and minute taker's copy of the agenda only.

Don't get into the habit of accepting late agenda items as this encourages late submissions. If you have planned your agenda carefully you will already have ensured that there is sufficient time for each agenda item. If you accept late agenda items you may need to drop something else from the agenda.

The best way to deal with late agenda items is to include them on the agenda for the next meeting. This will encourage people to submit their requests on time.

My final word on issuing the agenda is - never issue the agenda at the start of the meeting. This doesn't give anyone chance to prepare for the meeting, and is almost guaranteed to affect the success of the meeting.

Exercise: Create an Agenda Template

There is a set sequence for presenting the agenda items, as discussed earlier in this chapter. How you choose to present your agenda is a matter of personal choice. To help you, most organisations opt for centring the header section and the title 'Agenda'. The remainder of the document is usually left justified.

Create an agenda template document that you can adapt for all your future meetings.

6. Meeting Preparation

You could just issue the agenda and then arrive at the meeting on the given date and time. If you're the minute taker I wouldn't recommend this approach as you won't be properly prepared. What's more you will put yourself under unnecessary pressure. Why would anyone want to do this when most people claim minute taking is not their favourite task?

Being properly prepared means less pressure on the day and some work has already been done. A win/win outcome for the minute taker.

6.1 Preparing for the Meeting

As the minute taker you have an essential role to play in the meeting. Preparing for the meeting will reduce your stress level and make the task easier during the meeting. Never underestimate the value of proper planning. Here are some things you should do before the meeting:

1. Read and understand the context of each agenda item

2. Talk to contributors to clarify any points you don't understand. You will find note taking much easier during the meeting if you understand the agenda item

3. Obtain a list of any technical terms likely to be used in the meeting

4. Confirm which style of minutes you will be creating. This will influence how many notes you take during the meeting

5. Ensure you have a copy of the minutes for signing (if required) and a copy of the minutes for personal use

6. Ensure you have a personal copy of every document that will be part of the meeting, for personal use

7. Ensure you have a supply of pens or pencils that you like writing with. If you have a pen you don't like writing with it will be a distraction

8. Prepare your notepad and ensure you have plenty of pages

9. Print a small selection of spare copies of the agenda, reports etc. At every meeting someone will come without these documents

Handy hint: If you understand the agenda item you will find it much easier to create concise notes during the meeting. If you don't understand the agenda item you will find note taking hard work.

If you feel more comfortable with a checklist here is an example you might like to use. Some of the tasks relate to the meeting secretary and others involve the minute taker. You might like to laminate your meeting checklist to create a wipe-clean surface. Use it with a marker pen for all future meetings.

Preparation/Task	Completed Y/N
Meeting room and refreshments (if required) booked	
Equipment booked (if required)	
All agenda items, reports and other papers received before the agenda is issued	
All attendees have been invited to the meeting	
Chairperson has confirmed his/her preferred style of agenda	
Draft agenda created	
Agenda approved by the chairperson	
Agenda, reports and other documents issued to all parties	
Reception notified of visitors and visitors parking spaces booked (if required)	
I am familiar with each agenda item	
I have obtained updates for each action from the previous meeting	
The chairperson/minute taker briefing is booked/has taken place	
The chairperson has confirmed the style of minutes	
Copy of agenda, reports and other documents for personal use printed	
Spare copy documents printed	
Copy of the minutes from previous meeting for personal use, and a copy for signing (if required)	
Prepared notepad, pens etc	

6.2 Chairperson's and Minute Taker's Briefing

It's good practice for the chairperson and minute taker to have a short briefing before the actual meeting. The day before is the ideal time for this briefing. Many chairmen/women don't make the time for this essential briefing; believing that it's an unnecessary waste of time. Wrong!

This meeting can be completed in the time it takes to drink a cup of coffee. It can make the difference between an efficient or an average to poor meeting. The purpose of this briefing is to ensure both parties are properly prepared. No chairperson likes nasty surprises during their meeting.

The purpose of this meeting is to discuss the following:

1. Any help or support either party may need during the meeting

2. Decide who will be responsible for time-keeping

3. Discuss the agenda items. Does the chairperson wish to be prompted regarding any of the agenda items?

4. Are there any contentious or sensitive items on the agenda? If so, the chairperson should explain how these should be minuted

5. Are you new to the role of minute taker? If so, ask the chairperson to dictate what should be minuted

6. Are there any updates on the matters arising? Ideally both parties should already have the updated actions from the last meeting

7. Make sure you know which style of minutes are required

8. Does the chairperson want a register for signing at the meeting?

9. Does the chairperson want a copy of the minutes to sign at the meeting?

Handy hint: It's common to be asked to create a register for formal meetings. It's not as common for business meetings.

Exercise: Planning the Meeting Quiz

Imagine yourself as the meeting secretary for one of your organisation's monthly meetings.

Instructions:

Answer the questions in this quiz to see how much you know about the meeting secretary's role. You will find the answers to this exercise in the 'Appendices' at the end of the book.

1. As the meeting secretary what tasks might you be asked to do?

2. Name the three styles of agenda. Which is most commonly used for business meetings?

3. In what order should the agenda items appear?

4. Should all the main agenda items be captured under a single heading of 'Main agenda items'? Yes/No

5. Should 'Apologies' be agenda item number 1? If not, why not?

6. Does the chairperson have to approve the agenda before it's issued?

7. What information should be included in the header section of the agenda?

8. What sets the objectives agenda apart from the other agenda styles?

9. What is different about the chairperson's agenda to the version issued to everyone else?

10. State the nine things the minute taker should do to prepare for the meeting

11. Is a chairperson's/minute taker's briefing session necessary for informal meetings? Yes/No

12. Summarise the purpose of the chairperson's/minute taker's briefing session

Now go to the 'Appendices' at the end of the book to see how you got on.

Exercise: Pre-meeting Review

Before you go any further you might like to do a short review of your current pre-meeting practice.

Instructions:

Consider the following questions:

1. Do you currently go through all the tasks identified in the preparing for the meeting section?

44

2. Do you and the chairperson always have a briefing session before formal and business meetings? If not, why not?

3. Is there anything about the planning stage you will do differently in future?

4. Is there anything you weren't aware of before reading this chapter?

Now you're ready for the meeting.

7. The Meeting

During the meeting you are part of the management team. Don't underestimate your role; this is a very important and responsible role. It's important that you and the chairperson work together as a team.

If lots of people are talking at once, or you can't keep up with the discussions during the meeting, speak up. Point out that you can only take satisfactory minutes if the discussions are clear and measured.

7.1 Before the Meeting Starts

As minute taker you are going to be busy throughout the meeting. Anything you can do in advance will help you once the meeting starts.

Before the meeting starts ensure your notepad is already prepared (see example below). This will save time and make the task of note taking more efficient. An A4 pad is absolutely ideal. Simply divide your notepad into four columns and write the following headings:

Column 1 - Lead (this column can be narrow as it's just for the initials of the person leading the discussion, in case of query)

Column 2 - Notes/Actions (make this the widest column as it will have most information)

Column 3 - Action Owner and Completion Date (this column can be fairly narrow as it will only have very limited information)

Column 4 - Extra Notes (this column is just in case the anything extra is added to this agenda item later in the meeting. Hopefully this column should rarely be used)

The other task you might like to do before the meeting starts is write a list of the names of all attendees. Next to their name write their initials. During the meeting just use the initials to identify people.

Lead	Notes/Actions	Action Owner Comp Date	Extra Notes

7.2 Terms for Formal Meetings

There are common meeting terms that are only used during formal meetings. I have included a list of these common terms.

Adjourn = A suggestion to postpone the meeting to a future date. The chairperson should agree the new date before everyone leaves the meeting room

Ad-hoc = A committee or group that is brought together for a specific task. This group will not have a regular meeting pattern

Advisory = A committee formed to give advice and/or recommendations. This committee cannot make binding decisions

Amendment = A change made to the minutes after they have been issued. This decision will be made when discussing the minutes of the previous meeting

Executive = A sub-committee with the power to make binding decisions on behalf of the entire committee/group. The executive is generally made up of the chairperson and other key personnel from the group

Motion = A formal proposal or recommendation from a member of the group. This usually requires a proposer and seconder before it can be voted on. Typically this is used at AGMs to elect or re-elect members. The proposer starts by saying "I move that..."

Note: all motions should be minuted. If possible, get the motions in writing before the meeting. This will make your role easier

Motion Defeated = The majority of members have voted against a motion. The chairperson, will announce the motion is defeated

Order of Business = A set procedure for very formal meetings. This is a term sometimes used by local authorities and trade unions

Plenary = This is a power that has been granted to a group with no limitation upon their power. They are permitted to make binding decisions on behalf of the group or organisation they are acting for

Point of Order = A discussion point that is made but is not relevant to the discussions. This term is used when one of the group wishes to be pedantic on a particular point or choice of words

Postal Votes = As the name suggests these are votes received via the post. Postal votes are only permitted if the constitution allows for them

Proxy = This is a vote made on behalf of a member who is absent. The absent member gives someone permission to cast their vote in their absence. Proxy votes are only permitted if the constitution allows for them

Quorum = The minimum number of members required for decisions made by the group to be binding. It's the chairperson's responsibility to know how many members are required for the group to be quorate. This is usually, but not always, a third of the group

Resolution = This is a decision to accept or reject a motion or suggestion from a member of the group. If the motion is passed it becomes a resolution

Rider = This is an addition to be made to a resolution once it has been passed by the members

Standing = A gathering of members who meet regularly

Standing Orders = Rules regarding how the meeting should be run

Sub-committee = A small committee from members of the group. A sub-committee is usually formed with a specific remit

Tabling Papers = These are documents that weren't circulated to the members prior to the meeting. The chairperson should discourage this as you probably haven't allowed extra time to read and deal with these documents

Voting Rights = This is how the voting is done at formal meetings. This can be 'voice vote, a show of hands or a ballot'. A ballot is often used for electing officers if there is more than one nomination

Note: in the event of a tied vote the chair has the casting vote. If there is a clear winner, without the need for a casting vote, the chairperson may decide not to vote

Waiver = A rule that can be invoked to allow a mistake (usually procedural) to be overlooked

7.3 Common Abbreviations

Discussions during meetings can be high energy with lots of input from different people. It's virtually impossible to have time to write every word in full during meetings so most minute takers adopt some shorthand. I have included the most common words and their abbreviation. You may prefer to create your own shorthand, but here is a starting point for you:

Accommodation = accom
Accounts = accts
Acknowledge = ack
Advertisement = ad
Appointment = apt
Approximately = approx
Business = bus
Committee = comm
Company = co
Develop = dev
Exercise = ex
Experience = exp
Full-time = f/t
Government = gov
Hours = hrs
Immediately = imm
Information = info
Miscellaneous = misc
Necessary - nec
Opportunity = opp
Organisation = org
Part-time = p/t
Possible = poss
Recommend = rec
Reference = ref
Responsible = resp
Secretary = sec
Separate = sep
Signature = sig
Sufficient = suff
Temporary = temp
Through = thru

Handy hint: Jargon should only be used in business meetings if it's absolutely necessary and all parties understand the terms being used. It's best practice to avoid jargon.

7.4 Note Taking

As minute taker your role starts as soon as the chairperson opens the meeting. While the chairperson is dealing with the housekeeping matters make a note of any attendees you haven't already recorded. It's essential that you have an accurate record of who was present and who was absent. Present, apologies and absent should be recorded separately.

The essential minute taking skill is not an ability to write fast, but the ability to capture the essence of what was discussed. There is generally no need to capture everything that is said during the meeting. If the chairperson wants a record of everything that is said he/she should make this clear before the meeting starts.

It's normal to have duplication and surplus notes from the meeting. Don't worry about this during the meeting; simply edit the notes afterwards. The most important information to capture is details of all the actions, action owners and completion dates. It's useful to have a summary of the discussion that took place, but these don't need to be hugely detailed notes.

If you are using the full or objectives agenda you will need to summarise the discussion relating to every sub-heading, not just a summary of the main heading. The minutes relating to a full or objectives agenda are often lengthy, but this is unavoidable.

The notes you take during the meeting may include personal comments, opinions, bias etc. None of these should appear in the minutes. If the meeting involves particularly important or controversial decisions you may like to ask the chairperson to confirm what he/she wants minuted.

If you don't understand something that needs to be minuted interrupt and ask for clarification. It's much easier to do this during the meeting than afterwards.

No matter how carefully the meeting has been planned sometimes the discussion will go back to an agenda item already dealt with. If you have an 'extra notes' column in your notepad you will be able to slot any additional comments in.

Otherwise you will have to write the extra notes in your notepad with an explanation regarding which agenda item they relate to. This is time consuming, and may mean you miss something important.

Handy hint: Good meeting notes include the speaker, a summary of the discussion, details of the actions, action owner and completion date. The speaker won't appear in the minutes but it's useful to have this information in case of query.

There are a few useful rules regarding note taking in meetings. These are:

1. Make as many notes as you feel you need. Remember we're all different so no two people will take the same amount of notes

2. Write bullet points; you don't have time to write full sentences

3. Make a note of who is leading the discussion or making relevant comments. This is just in case of query after the meeting

4. Capture the message of the discussion, not a word-for-word account. The only exception is meetings where you've been asked to capture everything word-for-word

5. If the chairperson forgets to confirm the action completion date, remind him/her before the meeting moves on. Action owners can't be chased if no completion date has been agreed

6. Identify the agenda item your notes relate to. It's harder to do this after the meeting

7. Confirm names, jargon etc you don't understand. It's better to ask than issue incorrect minutes

8. If an argument ensues at the meeting take care not to capture the emotion. Only record the discussion, as you would normally

9. At all times keep the Freedom of Information Act in mind. This is particularly important if there is any possibility of your minutes being read by anyone outside the organisation

Finally, keep a copy of the agenda in front of you. You will probably need to refer to it frequently throughout the meeting.

Exercise: Note Taking Exercise

The purpose of this exercise is to give you experience of taking notes from a discussion that is taking place. Imagine the following discussion is taking place between the chairperson, Annie and Charlie.

Instructions:

1. Read the script twice to make sure you understand it thoroughly

2. If you were in a meeting listening to this discussion what notes would you make from this discussion? There are no right or wrong answers to this question. Note taking is a matter of personal choice so summarise what information you would feel comfortable with

3. Now you've created your notes convert them into summary minutes. Your summary should be a maximum of five sentences.

Chair: Charlie, the next agenda item is the drinks machines. I believe you wanted this item added to the agenda for today's meeting

Charlie: Yes, thank you. Last week I visited a new supplier – excellent meeting by the way.

Mita Sandhu is really clued up and keen to do business with us. Anyway, after the usual pleasantries, Mita pointed to a flashy new drinks machine and told me to help myself to anything I wanted. It offers various strengths of tea and coffee, black, white, sugar, no sugar etc, and was so much quicker than a kettle. It also dispenses cold water and other cold drinks

Annie: I've seen them; they're very good

Chair: Particularly for us non-coffee drinkers

Charlie: Anyway, I thought they would be a good idea for our meeting rooms

Annie: Excellent idea. Let's go ahead

Chair: What's the cost?

Charlie: Oh, I don't think it's too much. Probably less than we spend on the bottled water we have now, and taking into account the amount of time spent in the kitchen making drinks for everyone

Annie: And at least the water will be chilled

Chair: Have you got any idea of the cost?

Charlie: Well not exactly, but I could find out if we're interested. I just wanted to see how everyone feels about it first. I'm sure it won't be too bad really

Chair: won't we use a lot more water?

Annie: I think we'll save money as we often have bottles with just one glass of water taken out and the rest is wasted when the meeting is finished

Chair: Who is going to be responsible for filling it up with water and cleaning it?

Charlie: The caretakers or cleaners could do it at the end of each day when they lock-up

Chair: Are we in favour of this idea in principle? Charlie, you will need to calculate how many machines we need and get the best price possible. Can we agree that if it's no more expensive than our current arrangement, Charlie can go ahead and buy them, but if they are going to cost us more than the current arrangements we will bring it back for discussion at the next meeting?

The conclusion of this discussion is:

Chair: Charlie, this seems to be an action point for you

Charlie: I'll ring the suppliers after I've costed our current arrangement and then do a price comparison. All being well, I will have them installed before our meeting next month

Annie: You'd better speak to the caretakers and cleaners before they're installed. We don't want to upset anyone

Charlie: Good thinking; I'll do that

7.5 Working Through the Agenda

Regardless of whether you are minute taking at a formal, business or informal meeting, the order of the agenda is the same. It's bad practice to deal with items in a different order to the agenda. The order for dealing with agenda items is:

Introductions and Welcome
The chairperson will use this agenda item to remind everyone of the purpose of the meeting and what needs to achieved. Often you won't be asked to record anything for this agenda item.

Some chairmen/women like to include a single sentence that says "the chairperson welcomed everyone to the meeting". Ask your chairman/woman what you should record in the minutes.

Part of this agenda item will involve recording who is present and who is missing. For the minutes, everyone should be identified under one of the following headings:

Present - these are the people who were invited and attended as expected

In attendance - these are the people who aren't normally present at the meeting. This includes, speakers, visitors, substitutes or non-board members at a formal meeting

Apologies - this is anyone who sent their apologies. This can be done in advance of the meeting, or via someone who is present at the meeting. Anyone who is on holiday or sick leave is deemed to have sent their apologies

Absent or did not attend - these are the people who haven't sent their apologies and haven't turned up for the meeting

Observers - not every business or informal meeting will have observers. Observers are more common at formal meetings. Public meetings, AGMs and shareholder meetings generally have too many observers to account for them individually.

For the minutes count the number of observers and record this in the minutes. Note: the press and members of the public should be counted separately. For example - members of the public 30 people, press 5 people.

All of this information must be accurate as it provides essential information for the audit trail.

Handy hint: For formal meetings, some organisations like to include a heading of 'In attendance'. This is used to record non-board members. Find out what your organisation's policy is. There is no need to include this heading for business meetings unless your organisation wishes to.

Declarations of Interest
It's good practice for the chairperson to canvass any declarations of interest as part of the welcome and introductions. Unfortunately, not all chairmen/women think to do this.

Internal meetings rarely involve declarations of interest. However, declarations of interest may be raised in meetings involving external parties, board meetings and commercial meetings.

If anyone declares a conflict of interest capture this for the minutes. If there are no declarations of interest, don't bother including this heading in the minutes.

Minutes of the Previous Meeting
The chairperson will ask everyone present to confirm the minutes are an accurate record of the previous meeting. If so, the chairperson can

formally adopt the minutes, which you will record in the minutes. Some organisations like to sign the minutes, not just approve them.

There are various ways of recording that the minutes have been accepted by the group. The most common ways of recording this information are:

The minutes of the meeting held on [date of the meeting] were approved

The minutes of the meeting held on [date of the meeting] were accepted as a true and accurate record

The minutes of the meeting held on [date of the meeting] were approved as a true and accurate record

The minutes of the meeting held on [date of the meeting] were signed

If the minutes are inaccurate this is the only opportunity to amend them. Everyone present needs to be in agreement with the proposed changes. Note: the minutes should not be amended for grammar or spelling mistakes. Make the necessary changes to the minutes

There are various ways to record the changes to the minutes. The most common ways of dealing with this are:

1. On the new minutes, under the heading 'Minutes of the previous meeting', create a sub-heading 'Amendments'. Type the details of the amendments. For example, "The training budget for the new financial year is £80,000 not £85,000". Then add the following note - The minutes of the meeting hold on [date] were amended and subsequently approved

2. File the original minutes with the handwritten amendments

3. Correct the original minutes. File the amended minutes with the original version of that were issued

Note: don't reissue the minutes from the previous meeting.

Matters Arising
You and the chairperson should already know what everyone is going to say during matters arising. If you already have this information you won't need to write notes during Matters arising.

The minutes should include an update for each action and the status. The status will be - completed, in hand (this means as good as done), new deadline (for tasks not yet completed) or no action taken.

In the case of no action taken, it's important to include the reason why the action hasn't been completed. Enter the new deadline and initials of the person responsible for the action. If the action is to be closed make a note along the lines of 'Action not completed. No further action required'.

If there are any new updates make a note of them for the minutes.

Exercise: Précis the Matters Arising

This exercise is designed to give you practice at dealing with matters arising. The following were the 'Matters arising' from our recent Dinosaurs 'R' Us Housing Group meeting.

As you can see the chairperson allowed each action owner to provide a very detailed explanation. Now you need to précis this information for the minutes.

Instructions:

1. Create a summary for the minutes regarding each of the matters arising

2. Create the Matters arising in the way you wish to present them in the minutes. Imagine this is part of your minutes document that will be issued to the attendees

You will find the answers to this exercise in the Appendices section at the end of the book. Compare your responses with the answers.

Matters Arising:
Neighbour dispute: There had been an ongoing dispute between Mrs Tyler (an elderly lady living alone) and the Cobb family (Mr and Mrs Cobb and their children Fred and Florence).

With some intervention from our Housing Officer, matters have now been resolved and the Cobb children will not play with their ball in the garden in future. The argument had been about the Cobb children's ball going into Mrs Tyler's garden regularly.

Fence falling down: The fence was falling down at 32 Rockhard Road. The fence has now been replaced as the damage was beyond economic repair. The repair was paid for by the Housing Association at a cost of £600. The tenants have been told they will be responsible for the ongoing maintenance of the fence.

Broken window: There is a broken window at 19 Boulder Boulevard. Mr and Mrs Stoneface have been instructed that they must replace the broken window, as the damage was caused by their nephew, Arthur, when he came to stay with them.

It has been made clear to Mr and Mrs Stoneface that the Dinosaurs 'R' Us Housing Association is not responsible for malicious damage. They have also been told that if they do not arrange the repair themselves, we will replace the broken window and the cost will be added to their rent. They have been given 3 weeks to sort this out.

Reports
If your meeting involves any reports or other documents be sure to attach a copy to the minutes. This will save the need to include detailed notes about the report or other document.

If there are no queries or actions regarding the report just make a note to this effect.

Main Agenda Items
The chairperson should deal with each main agenda item in the order they appear on the agenda. For your notes summarise the discussion and who the main speaker is, in case of query after the meeting. Also note the actions, action owner(s) and target date for completing the action.

If there are any supporting documents that formed part of the discussion attach a copy to the minutes.

Any Other Business
If the chairperson manages their meetings correctly you will rarely have to make any notes for any other business. The matters discussed under any other business should be urgent items that came to light after the agenda was issued.

Sometimes there will be nothing to record in the minutes. If in doubt, ask the chairperson to clarify whether they want the item minuted of not. If so, treat these items in the same way as the main agenda items. Your notes and actions will appear under 'Any Other Business' in the minutes.

7.6 Recording the Actions

Actions can only be allocated to someone present at the meeting. There is no mechanism for reporting the outcome otherwise. The action owner may choose to delegate the task to someone who didn't attend the meeting. This is fine, but they can't abdicate responsibility for owning the action.

As far as the minutes are concerned the action owner remains the person present at the meeting. He/she will be responsible for ensuring the action is completed and reporting the update at the next meeting.

Although the action may be delegated to someone who isn't present at the meeting they are not automatically entitled to a copy of the minutes. It's the action owner's responsibility to share the details of the action with the person who will do the work.

If there are no actions from a particular discussion summarise the discussion in the usual way. Add a note stating that there were no actions from the agenda item. This will be helpful to anyone reading the minutes at a later date.

When agreeing the actions for each agenda item make sure there is an action owner and completion date. It's important that everyone understands what they are expected to do and when. Without an action owner and completion date it will be difficult to make anyone accountable for the actions at the next meeting.

Some organisations like to create a table of actions as well as the minutes. Here's an example you might like to use:

No	Action	Action Owner	Update For The Next meeting

The table of actions can be useful when the meeting secretary or minute taker is obtaining updates on the actions for the next meeting. Some chairmen/women find this document useful when dealing with matters arising at the next meeting.

Handy hint: Don't allow the meeting to move forward until the action owner and completion date have been agreed. You will struggle to sort this out after the meeting.

Exercise: Record the Actions

Our local town has a Tourism Committee. This committee meets monthly to discuss ways to increase the revenue the local economy receives from tourism. The group is keen to involve more businesses as this is good for the local economy and the town's residents. Below you will find the actions agreed at our recent meeting.

Instructions:

1. Create a document to record each action from our meeting. Imagine you are creating these actions for your notepad, not the minutes document

2. Just capture the information you need for your notes. You will need this information to create the minutes later on

3. You will find the answers to this exercise in the Appendices section at the end of the book. Compare what your have written with the answers

Actions:

All of these actions will be completed before the next meeting. The group is meeting four weeks from today so you can add the date.

1. We need to increase the membership of group. We want to engage more local businesses to help us promote tourism in the town. This will spread the cost to each business involved and potentially benefit everyone who lives in the town. Tivon Quigley has agreed to create a letter that can be sent to all local business owners. He will create a draft letter for discussion and approval at the next meeting

2. We want as many local restaurants and cafés to get involved in a discount voucher scheme. Yaffa Auld, Ava Chan and Ziv Singh have agreed to compile a list of potential businesses to approach

3. The local theatre has offered to put on a special event to celebrate International Women's Day. This event will include a meal, drinks, performance, meet the cast and a talk by the new Artistic Director. Adeline Galbraith has agreed to act as our primary point of contact, and will work with the theatre to promote this event. Ethan Schmidt will arrange a press release to promote the event

4. Our website is looking a little tired. Yachne Dabney has agreed to get some quotes for a new logo. Doron Gwin will come up with some new text for the website. We will discuss this at the next meeting and agree the website changes

You will find the answers to this exercise in the Appendices section at the end of the book.

7.7 Other Ways to Record Minutes

There are other ways to record meetings. Personally, I believe minute taking is still an effective method of providing an accurate record of a meeting. I'll leave you to decide the option for your meetings.

If the chairperson decides to record your meetings it's important to obtain the express permission of everyone present. It's not acceptable to just assume the consent is given just because people have attended the meeting.

Recording Meetings
In this high-tech age it may seem logical to use electronic recording equipment to record your meeting. With good quality recording equipment and a disciplined group, recording your meeting is a viable option.

There's nothing to stop you recording your meeting. However, bear in mind the recording equipment will record everything that was discussed. This will include comments you might not want recorded.

Most meetings involve more than one person speaking at once. The recording equipment will pick up every voice and other noise (e.g. clattering tea cups). After the meeting it may be difficult to identify who was talking. Anyone listening to the recording after the meeting may struggle to follow the discussion. This may render the recording valueless.

If for any reason the electronic equipment fails you will have no record and no audit trail for the meeting. If you are happy to risk not having a record of your meeting this is fine.

If you don't want to record the entire meeting you could record a summary and the actions. In this case, have the discussion in the usual way.

At the end of the discussion the chairperson should summarise the discussion, action, action owner and completion date. Note: this is almost certain to slow the meeting down.

Using a Laptop Computer
Using a laptop computer might seem like a good idea as you can type as you go, and so save time producing the minutes after the meeting. It's

true that many of us can type faster than we write. However, before rushing for the laptop, consider the following:

Discussions often drift backwards and forwards. You will need to type the notes as the conversation goes. At the end of the meeting you will need to cut and paste the information into the correct part of the document. You won't have time search the relevant part of the document during the meeting.

If you opt to type your notes in the meeting you will end up with far more notes than necessary. Be prepared to delete a large chunk of the notes you create. Editing often takes longer than starting from scratch. You should factor in up to 50% more time for the editing process.

If you are going to type the minutes during the meeting save a copy of the document before you start cutting and pasting after the meeting.

You should also be aware that attendees often find someone typing a distraction. I'm not suggesting you shouldn't type notes for this reason; just that you should be aware of it.

A final word of caution, if you are going to type the notes, you might like to arrange for someone to take written notes as a back-up plan. It's very easy to accidentally delete or lose a document and then have no record at all of the meeting.

Apps

I couldn't write a book about minute taking without including something on apps. Nowadays there really is an app for everything in business, including minute taking. With so many apps to sift through, it can be hard to separate the useful from the gimmicky.

My initial intention was to do the research for you, but then I realised this is an impossible task. There are so many business apps available now that I would end up writing an entire book on the subject. Therefore, I shall leave you to do your own research.

Some traditionalists feel there is no room for apps in meetings. Others believe apps are the way forward and we should all embrace them wholeheartedly. Personally, I feel that we are all individual and should choose the option that works best for us.

You might like to try some apps and see how you get on. In your chosen search engine type the details of what you want the app to do. For example - type "apps for creating minutes".

Handy hint: If you decide to type or record the minutes ask someone to make hand written notes. This will provide a back-up in case of technology failure.

8. The Minutes

The minutes are not a stand-alone document. The minutes need to mirror the agenda document in style, presentation and content. This is why I haven't made this book about minute taking only.

Minutes are a valuable part of meetings. They provide an accurate record of the business of the meeting. They are also used to record actions, identify the action owner and the completion date. Most people have limited interest in the minutes so make sure they are well presented and easy to read.

Many organisations have no rules regarding minutes and offer very little guidance. How do you know whether you should be typing summary, verbatim or action point minutes? By understanding each type of minutes you will be able to suggest the best option for your organisation or meeting.

Formal and business meetings always have minutes. You may choose not to create formal minutes for an informal meeting but you should still have some notes from the meeting. Otherwise you have no record of what was discussed or agreed.

Handy hint: It's important that your minutes are written in plain English. You will find lots of really useful information on the Plain English Campaign website. The website address is - www.plainenglish.co.uk

8.1 Styles of Minutes

There are three styles of minutes. These are summary, verbatim and action point minutes. In theory any style of agenda can be used with any style of minutes. In reality it's highly unlikely that you will ever find action point minutes with a full agenda or an objectives agenda.

It's important to know your organisation's preferred style of minutes. If there is no policy you or the chairperson can choose the style that you feel most comfortable with. Note: for most business meetings summary minutes are the preferred choice.

Summary Minutes
Summary minutes are the most commonly used style of minutes. They provide more information than action point minutes but less than verbatim minutes. Summary minutes capture the essential information, but as briefly as possible. This style of minutes is suitable for most business meetings.

Summary minutes follow the headings and numbering of the agenda (basic, full or objectives agenda). If the minutes are being used with a basic agenda, you can present the summary in any order you wish.

If the minutes are being used with a full or objectives agenda the summary should follow the order of the sub-headings on the agenda. This will ensure the minutes tie up with the agenda accurately.

Prior to the meeting, the chairperson and minute taker should agree the level of detail that should appear in summary minutes. This may help you to decide how many notes you need to take during the meeting.

Verbatim Minutes
In this case verbatim does not automatically mean word-for-word. Generally, it means everything that was discussed during the meeting. If the chairman/woman wants a word-for-word record of the meeting he/she should state this at the start of the meeting.

Verbatim minutes are often used for disciplinary hearings or meetings following a health and safety incident.

Verbatim minutes can make the minute taker's task challenging; especially if the discussion drifts backwards and forwards. This style of minutes works best if you have a very disciplined chairperson who can keep the discussions focused and moving forwards.

Allow at least 50% more time to create verbatim minutes. Expect a very lengthy set of minutes if you are creating verbatim minutes with the full or objectives agenda. This is unavoidable.

Action Point Minutes
These are hardly minutes at all. This style of minutes comprises the headings from the agenda followed by the action, action owner and completion date.

Action point minutes are only really used for informal meetings or project meetings where you meet daily/weekly and just require an update. Most organisations feel these minutes provide insufficient information for business meetings.

If you have an agenda item without any actions just make a note that there are no actions. This ensures you have an accurate audit trail for the meeting.

8.2 Layout of the Minutes

By varying the font size for different parts of the document you make it easier for the reader to spot what they are looking for. Here are my suggestions for your minutes document:

Name of the group or meeting - Arial 14 or 16 point bold text

Date and start time of the meeting - Arial 12 point bold text

Venue - Arial 12 point bold text

Document title e.g. Minutes of [group/meeting name] - Arial 14 or 16 point bold text

Main headings - Arial 12 point bold text

Sub-headings (full and objectives agenda) - Arial 11 point bold text

Notes that makes up the minutes - Arial 11 point text

Details of actions - Arial 11 point italic text

Name of the action owner - Arial 10 point bold text

Completion date for actions - Arial 10 point text

All minutes, regardless of style, should have a header and the same numbering/headings as the agenda. This information makes it easy to audit both documents in future.

It's not necessary to include the finish time of your meeting, although some chairmen/women like to do so. Ask the chairperson if they want to include the finish time.

The header section of your minutes document should contain the following information:

Name of the group that is meeting

Date and start time of the meeting

Venue (full meeting address)

Leave at least two blank lines after the header section. The white space helps to make the document visually appealing and easy to read.

If you centred the header on your agenda document you should do the same thing for the minutes. Equally, if you left justified the header section (as per the example above) on your agenda document then this is how the header for your minutes document should appear.

Underneath the header section you should identify who was present and who was absent from the meeting. This information is not numbered, as it wasn't numbered on the agenda. Numbering this information would make the numbering of the two documents out of sync. Present and absent should be recorded as follows:

Present: The chairperson should be listed first, followed by the minute taker. After this it's a matter of personal choice how you list the attendees. The simplest way to do this is to list everyone present in alphabetical order by last name. Note: if you randomly list attendees you will find the person at the bottom of the list often takes offence as they think this makes them less important.

Handy hint: If you have a lot of attendees for your meeting you may like to list them in two columns to use less space

Apologies: Apologies can be submitted anytime up to the start of the meeting. Anyone on annual leave or absent due to sickness is deemed to have sent their apologies.

Absent: It's important to identify these people separately as you need an accurate record for audit purposes.

Observers: Most business meetings won't have observers. If you don't have any observers at your meeting don't bother with this heading.

Strictly speaking, you don't need to name observers as they haven't contributed to the meeting. You may choose to name the observer. In the case of public meetings e.g. AGM's there are often too many observers to name them. In which case write observers and the total number of observers.

If you have members of the press present at your meeting they should be recorded separately to the other observers. In this case after 'Observers' write another heading for 'Press' and the number or journalists present. Once again, they are not named in the minutes.

Handy hint: No one likes to be identified as 'Absent'. If some attendees are poor at sending their apologies and simply don't turn up for meetings this might stop this behaviour pattern.

Formal meetings are treated slightly differently. If you have non-board members present at the meeting, most organisations like to list these attendees under a separate heading of 'In attendance'.

If anyone attended the meeting for a single agenda item make a note of this. The simplest way to record this is to write the person's name and the agenda item in brackets. Although this may seem pedantic it does ensure you have an accurate record of your meeting for audit purposes.

Find out whether your chairman/woman wants to include the finish time of the meeting in the minutes.

8.3 Examples of Minutes Documents

Below is a typical example of how those present and absent might appear in your minutes. This part of the document will be the same whether you chose a basic, full or objectives agenda.

Minutes of the [group name] meeting
Held on [date and start time of the meeting]
At [meeting address]

Present:
[Name] Chairperson
[Name] Minute taker
[Name] List the attendees in alphabetical order by last name
[Name]

Apologies:
[Name] List these in alphabetical order by last name
[Name]

Absent:
[Name] List these in alphabetical order by last name
[Name]

Leave at least two blank lines after this information. The white space helps to make the document visually appealing and easy to read.

The layout of the rest of the document should match the style and numbering you used in the agenda document. Below I have included examples of how the rest of your minutes document might look.

Personally, I think it's important to make the actions stand out from the minutes. This helps the action owners easily identify their actions. It also makes it easier for the meeting secretary when getting updates on outstanding actions.

White space on your document is important as it makes the minutes easier to read. Before anyone reads the content of the minutes they will do a visual check first. If the document doesn't look visually appealing the reader is likely to just scan, rather than read, the document.

Example of Minutes Using a Basic Agenda
Here is an example of the rest of the minutes when used with a basic agenda.

Minutes of the [group name] meeting
Held on [date and start time of the meeting]
At [meeting address]

1. Welcome, introductions and administration
Summary of anything the chairperson wants minuted

2. Minutes of the previous meeting
The minutes of the meeting held on [date of the meeting] were approved

3. Matters arising
Maternity cover for Sukhi Patel - Summary.
Replacement scheme manager for Redrock Place – Summary
Resolve anti-social behaviour issues with the tenant at 10 Parsons Lane - Summary

4. Reports
Attach a copy of the reports to the minutes. This means you don't need to create a summary of each report. Just minute any comments made during the meeting.
Finance Report - Comments
Company Risk Assessment - Comments

5. Official opening of the Sun Rising Village Development by Barrie Boulder MP
Summary
Details of the actions
Action owner(s) Completion date

6. Any other business

7. Date of next meeting
Date and time agreed for the next meeting

Example of Minutes Using a Full Agenda
Here is an example of the rest of the minutes when used with a full agenda.

Minutes of the [group name] meeting
Held on [date and start time of the meeting]
At [meeting address]

1. Welcome, introductions and administration (or a variation on this)
Summary of anything the chairperson wants minuted

2. Minutes of the previous meeting
The minutes of the meeting held on [date of the meeting] were approved

3. Matters arising
3.1 Maternity cover for Sukhi Patel - Summary
3.2 Replacement scheme manager for Redrock Place – Summary
3.3 Resolve anti-social behaviour issues with the tenant at 10 Parsons Lane - Summary

4. Reports
Attach a copy of the reports to the minutes. This means you don't need to create a summary of each report. Just minute any comments made during the meeting. For completeness you may choose to add a note that says a copy of the reports are attached.
4.1 Finance Report - Comments
4.2 Company Risk Assessment - Comments

5. Official opening of the Sun Rising Village Development by Barrie Boulder MP
5.1 Timetable for visit
Summary
Details of the action
Action owner Completion date

5.2 Duties Barrie Boulder will perform
Summary
Details of the action
Action owner Completion date

5.3 Publicity for the event
Summary
Details of the action
Action owner Completion date

5.4 Security issues
Summary
Details of the action
Action owner Completion date

6. Any other business

7. Date of next meeting
Date and time agreed for the next meeting

Example of Minutes Using an Objectives Agenda
Here is an example of the rest of the minutes when used with an objectives agenda.

Minutes of the [group name] meeting
Held on [date and start time of the meeting]
At [meeting address]

1. Welcome, introductions and administration (or a variation on this)
Summary of anything the chairperson wants minuted

2. Minutes of the previous meeting
The minutes of the meeting held on [date of the meeting] were approved

3. Matters arising
3.1 To provide an update on the maternity cover for Sukhi Patel - Summary
3.2 To appoint a replacement scheme manager for Redrock Place – Summary
3.3 To provide an update on the anti-social behaviour issues with the tenant at 10 Parsons Lane - Summary

4. Reports
Attach a copy of the reports to the minutes. This means you don't need to create a summary of each report. Just minute any comments made during the meeting.
4.1 To receive the finance report from FF
4.2 To receive the group's updated risk assessment from RC
4.3 To receive the training budget and plans for the current financial year report from MM

5. Official opening of the Sun Rising Village Development by Barrie Boulder MP
5.1 To finalise the timetable for visit
Summary
Details of the actions
Action owner Completion date

5.2 To discuss the duties Barrie Boulder will perform
Summary
Details of the actions
Action owner Completion date

5.3 To agree the publicity for the event
Summary
Details of the actions
Action owner Completion date

5.4 To discuss the security issues
Summary
Details of the actions
Action owner Completion date

6. Any other business

7. Date of next meeting
Date and time agreed for the next meeting

Exercise: Create a Minutes Template

Create a minutes template that you can use for future meetings.

Instructions:

1. Before you create your minutes template review your agenda template

2. The header section must match the style used for your agenda template

3. Did you opt for a basic, full or objectives agenda? Ensure the style and numbering matches in both documents

8.4 Creating the Minutes

So, the meeting is over and you're faced with pages of notes. Now you need to convert these into clear, concise and accurate minutes. This task may seem daunting initially, but it's not as difficult as it first appears.

When creating the minutes there are a few rules. If you bear these in mind you will find the task easier:

1. The minutes must be a factual record of the discussion. This is not an opportunity to use your personal writing style

2. Keep the sentences as short (less than 20 words) and clear as possible

3. Write the minutes in the third person. There should be no reference to 'I, we, you, or your'

4. Keep the minutes succinct but without leaving important information out. Minute taking will definitely develop your précis skills

5. For summary minutes try to keep the summary to less than five sentences

6. If you used a full or objectives agenda write a couple of sentences to summarise the main heading. Then create one to two sentences for each sub-heading. The less you write the better as people won't read lengthy minutes

7. The numbering on your minutes document must match the numbering on the agenda

Handy hint: The minutes need to make sense to anyone who wasn't at the meeting. This doesn't mean the reader needs to understand the full discussion that took place.

There are some common phrases that often appear in minutes. Here are some typical examples to get you started. You don't need to use these examples they are just a starting point to help you when creating your minutes.

The meeting agreed that...
The meeting decided to...
The meeting resolved...
It was proposed that...
The meeting discussed...
The chairperson, finance director etc outlined new proposals for...
The marketing team will...
The chairperson suggested that...
A meeting is to be arranged to...
The chairperson informed the meeting that...
It was agreed that...

Concerns were expressed that...

If no decision was reached regarding an agenda item, record this in the minutes. For example 'no decision was reached'. This should be followed by a note that explains what happens next. For example - a sub-group will be set up to discuss the matter and come up with a proposal. This will be presented at the next meeting.

Note: even if you create summary minutes with a full or objectives agenda, the minutes will be a lengthy document.

Handy hint: The longer your putt off writing the minutes the more time-consuming the task will be as it becomes difficult to remember what was discussed.

Exercise: To Minute or Not

This exercise is designed to help you decide what should and shouldn't be minuted.

Instructions:

Read the two scenarios below and then answer the questions relating to each scenario.

Scenario 1:
During a board (formal) meeting a contentious motion is passed by the members. After a lengthy debate the majority agreed to dismiss a senior member of staff. This senior member of staff is not present at the board meeting.

One of the board members is very unhappy with the decision. He demands that his negative vote is recorded in the minutes. He also wants his reasons for voting against the motion to be recorded word-for-word. Finally, he wants to be named in the minutes.

Answer the following questions:

1. Should the member's comments be recorded word-for-word?

2. Should the member's name be included in the minutes?

3. What should be minuted if you decide not to record the comments word-for-word?

Scenario 2:
You are chairing a multi-departmental (business) meeting involving several senior managers.

One of the groups brings a written statement to the meeting. In it she is very critical of another group member. Her statement raises doubt about her colleague's honesty, integrity, motives and competence in the role. The statement is not only critical, it also contains unsubstantiated allegations. The member is asking for her statement to be included in the minutes.

Answer the following questions:

1. Should the written statement be attached to the minutes?

2. If you decide not to include the statement what should be minuted?

3. Who decides what should go into the minutes?

You will find the answers to this exercise in the Appendices section at the end of the book.

8.5 Approving and Issuing the Minutes

Although you have done all the work, the chairperson is the owner of this document. The chairperson should approve the minutes before you issue them.

Create a full set of draft minutes before issuing them to the chairperson for review and approval. To ensure your minutes are ready for approval, use the following checklist:

1. Each agenda item includes a summary of the discussion (unless you are creating action point minutes)

2. The minutes are written in the third person, and there is no reference to individual contributors

3. The minutes are written in clear and concise English

4. The minutes include details of all the actions

5. Every action has an action owner

6. Every action has a completion date

7. Anyone who wasn't present will have an appreciation of what was discussed

If the chairperson fails to approve the minutes within five working days of the meeting, go ahead and issue the minutes. If there are any inaccuracies these will have to be dealt with at the next meeting.

If the minutes aren't issued some of the actions won't be completed.

8.6 Who Should Have a Copy of the Minutes?

Anyone who was invited to the meeting is automatically entitled to a copy of the minutes. This includes those people who sent apologies or failed to attend.

Anyone who wasn't invited to the meeting must seek the chairperson's permission. This is regardless of their seniority in the organisation. If anyone asks you to send them a copy of the minutes ask them to contact the chairperson.

If the minutes contain sensitive or confidential information the chairperson may decide to exercise his/her discretion and only issue the minutes to regular attendees. If the minutes do contain sensitive or confidential information include a note to this effect in the covering email.

Once the minutes have been issued do not make any changes until the next meeting. It's common for attendees to send comments or ask the minutes to be amended, but the answer is always 'NO'.

Handy hint: Although minutes are a factual account of the meeting they shouldn't be unduly long. Don't feel compelled to write too many notes, or use all the notes you take during the meeting.

Once the minutes have been issued your role is finished until the next meeting. The task of following up on the actions becomes the responsibility of the meeting secretary for the next meeting.

Exercise: Create Summary Minutes From Your Notes

In chapter 7 you were asked to record the actions from our local Tourism Committee meeting.

Instructions:

1. Create the summary minutes and actions from the Record the Actions exercise in chapter 7. You can only use the information you captured in your notes

2. Present the minutes exactly as you would if these were minutes for one of your own meetings. Note: this may mean you have missing information

You will find the answers to this exercise in the Appendices section at the end of the book. Compare what your have written with the answers

Exercise: Creating Minutes Review

You now know the good practice regarding minutes. Use this opportunity to do a short review of your current working practices and decide what you are going to do differently in future.

Instructions:

Answer the following questions.

1. Do you currently follow all the good practice guidelines mentioned in this chapter?

2. Have you identified any improvements you can make to your own minutes? If so, what are these?

3. Do you think you will take less notes in future?

4. Which style of minutes are you most likely to use in future?

5. What have you learnt about creating minutes that you didn't already know?

6. Are you going to find minute taking easier in future?

7. Do you feel more confident about minute taking?

9. Freedom of Information Act

The Freedom of Information Act 2000 gives UK citizens the right to ask any public body for all the information they have on any subject they choose. The Freedom of Information (Scotland) Act 2002 covers the public bodies that the Holyrood parliament has jurisdiction over.

The Freedom of Information and Privacy Act is the United States equivalent. For other countries type the following and select the country from the list available:

https://en.wikipedia.org/wiki/Freedom_of_information_laws_by_country

The media frequently uses this right to obtain information that forms the basis of news stories. Unless there is a good reason not to, the organisation must provide the information within 20 working days.

Anyone can make a request for information, and you can ask for any information you like. There are no restrictions on age, nationality or where you live. Some information may be withheld to protect various interests that are allowed by the Act. If information is withheld the public authority must tell you why they have not shared this information.

You can also ask for any personal information the organisation holds about you. If you ask for information about yourself, then your request will be dealt with under the Data Protection Act 1998.

From a minute taker's point of view the Freedom of Information Act and the Data Protection Act can present a major challenge. When creating minutes carefully consider how much information should be recorded (particularly if you work in the public sector).

9.1 The Public Sector

If you work in the public sector be aware of the impact the Freedom of Information Act may have on your role. We are only dealing with the Act in respect of meetings and minute taking. You will need to do your own research to find out how the Act impacts your role more broadly.

The Freedom of Information Act applies to all public bodies. These include:

1. Government departments. The list is extensive. Type 'How to make a freedom of information request' into your search engine for details of the departments

2. Local authorities and councils

3. Schools colleges and universities

4. Health trusts, hospitals and doctors' surgeries

5. Publicly owned companies

6. Publicly funded museums

7. The police

9.2 What is Covered by the Freedom of Information Act?

The Freedom of Information Act requires every public authority to have a 'publication scheme'. This has to be approved by the Information Commissioner's Officer (ICO), and has to include the information covered by the scheme.

In short, this scheme means that certain classes of information must be routinely available to the public. This includes policies and procedures, minutes of meetings, annual reports and financial information.

If you would like to know more about what is covered by the Freedom of Information Act, please refer to the Information Commissioner's website (http://ico.org.uk).

9.3 Exempt Information

As I've already stated anyone can request information held by a public authority. This doesn't mean you will always receive all the information you ask for though. If there is a good reason to refuse the request, some information can be withheld.

There are three reasons why public authorities may refuse an entire request. These reasons are:

1. It would cost too much or take too many staff to deal with the request

2. The request is deemed to be vexatious

3. The request repeats a previous request from the same person

There are also various reasons for a public authority only providing limited information. If you would like to know more please refer to the Information Commissioner's website (http://ico.org.uk).

Even though you may not have to disclose a full copy of your minutes do take care when minuting discussions.

9.4 Useful Websites

If you work in a role where your meetings and minutes may be subject to the Freedom of Information Act you may find the following websites helpful.

The Freedom of Information Act:

United Kingdom - http://www.gov.uk

Scotland - http://www.scotland.gov.uk

United States - http://www.foia.gov/

The Information Commission:

United Kingdom - http://www.ico.gov.uk/

Scotland - http://www.itspublicknowledge.info

United States Information Agency - http://www.dosfan.lib.uic.edu/usia/

Handy hint: If your minutes contain confidential information make a reference indicating where this can be found. If you receive a freedom of information request you will be able to identify and remove the confidential information easily.

10. Conclusion

Creating the minutes should not be viewed as a stand-alone task. It's closely linked to the agenda in respect of layout and presentation.

The task of minute taking will be made easier or more difficult by the skills of the chairperson. Unfortunately, you have no control over this. You can reduce the pressure on yourself by gathering as much information as possible ahead of the meeting. Also, try not to capture everything that is discussed during the meeting. Learn to just capture the important points.

Here is a useful reminder about minutes:

1. Type the minutes as soon as possible after the meeting, definitely within two working days. The sooner you type the minutes the easier you will find this task

2. It's best to deal with any queries relating to the meeting whilst everyone can remember what was said. If possible, deal with queries during the meeting

3. When creating the minutes think of the Freedom of Information Act. The minutes should be suitable for anyone outside the meeting to read them

4. The minutes should be a factual and non-biased précis of the discussions that took place

5. Most people wait for the minutes before completing their actions. They often rely on the minutes to tell them what their actions are

6. If the minutes are not issued in a timely manner they may not be read at all

7. The attendees may not be capable of producing good quality minutes themselves but they will be quick to spot errors

Hopefully by now you feel confident as a meeting secretary or minute taker. You might like to try this quiz to test your knowledge.

Exercise: Agenda and Minute Taking Quiz

1. When should you issue the agenda for a monthly, or less frequent, meeting?

a) At the start of the meeting   b) With the minutes from the previous meeting   c) At least four working days before the meeting - circle your answer

2. Name the three styles of agenda

3. Which style of agenda is no longer commonly used?

4. Who is responsible for creating the agenda?

5. Does the agenda always have to be approved before it's issued?

6. Name the three categories of meeting

7. Why does the chairperson have a different agenda to everyone else? What is different about it?

8. Who creates the chairperson's agenda?

a) The chairperson   b) The Meeting Secretary   c) Someone else entirely - circle your answer

9. How many notes should you take during the meeting?

10. What information should you capture regarding the actions?

11. What should you do if the chairperson doesn't confirm the details of the actions?

12. Name the three different styles of minutes

13. Which style of minutes is most commonly used for business meetings?

14. Who owns the minutes?

a) The minute taker   b) The chairperson   c) the group - circle your answer

15. Does the chairperson always need to approve the minutes before they are issued?

You will find the answers to these questions in the Appendices section.

Finally, I have created a case study that you might also like to work through.

Exercise: Minute Taker's Case Study

Overview:

You have recently started working at 'The Only Way Is Up Ltd'; a business consultancy that employs 40 staff. You are employed as the PA to the Chief Executive. He formed the company five years ago.

The Chief Executive confirmed that he's an experienced meetings chairman and attendee. He recognises that good practice protocols exist but accepts that he doesn't always implement them. Some of his team don't know that protocol exists for meetings and minute taking.

Each month the Chief Executive has a meeting with his two fellow Directors, the Sales and Marketing Manager and 10 Sales and Marketing Consultants. The Chief Executive is always the chairman of this meeting. The aim of this meeting is to review how the business is getting on. The objectives for each meeting are:

1. Focus on existing customers (identify if we've lost any customers since the last meeting)

2. Is there anything we could have done to keep them?

3. Discuss new customers gained since the last meeting

4. Identify potential new customers

5. Consider ways to raise our profile and market ourselves better

As part of the meeting the group discusses customer queries, sales techniques that are or aren't working, and any areas of weakness in terms of performance. This is used to move the business forward.

This is your first meeting. You're an observer at this meeting so you can see how they operate. The Chief Executive has asked for your feedback at the end of the meeting. As a fresh pair of eyes, he thinks you may be able to see things they don't see.

The departing PA is the minute taker for this meeting. She is an excellent shorthand secretary and prides herself on her ability to capture everything that is said.

Attendees:

Chief Executive - Dennis Jackson (DJ)
Outgoing PA - Pamela Partridge (PP)
Director - Sara Higgins (SH)
Finance Director - Freddie Fiscal (FF)

Sales and Marketing Manager - Alexandros Stavros (AS)
Sales and Marketing Consultant - Rajesh Kumani (RK)
Sales and Marketing Consultant - Poppy Frankenstone (PF)
Sales and Marketing Consultant - Betty-Jean McBricker (BJM)
Sales and Marketing Consultant - Melville Muchrocks (MM)
Sales and Marketing Consultant - Lan Patel (LP)
Sales and Marketing Consultant - Hazel Sheppard (HS)
Sales and Marketing Consultant - Hugo Williams (HW)
Sales and Marketing Consultant - Sachiko Jaggers (SJ)
Sales and Marketing Consultant - Ricky Cobblehoff (RC)
Sales and Marketing Consultant - John Rockhead (JR)

Actions:
The actions agreed during this meeting were:

1. We've lost one of our oldest clients in the last month. They said they could no longer afford our services. AS has an action to speak to them and see if we can get them back again

2. Everyone is to bring last month's and this month's sales reports to the next meeting

3. Each of the Sales Consultants has been asked to come up with a plan for getting three new clients before the end of the year. Alexandros Stavros is to work with the team and create an action plan for discussion at the next meeting

Your observations:
Your observations from the meeting are:

1. The chairman arrived 10 minutes late. No-one commented or seemed to mind

2. As the chairman was late he skipped the 'Welcome and administration' agenda item. He was keen to make up some of the lost time

3. The agenda was handed out at the start of the meeting

4. Melville Muchrocks and Lan Patel didn't turn up, but didn't send their apologies either. No one knew why they were absent. Everyone else was present

5. Two errors were found in last month's minutes. The minute taker made a hand-written note on her copy of the previous minutes. She didn't record this in the minutes for today's meeting

6. The chairman signed the copy with the hand-written amendments

7. Various conversations were going on during the meeting. The chairman ignored this. The attendees talking amongst themselves made the task of minute taking hard work

8. Most of the attendees had forgotten to bring copies of last month's sales reports. The chairman decided to adjourn this item until the next meeting

9. Part way through the meeting Pamela, the outgoing PA, was asked to serve coffee. No-one took any notes while this was happening so there was a gap in the notes for the minutes

10. One of Ricky Cobblehoff's actions from last month's meeting hasn't been completed. There was no satisfactory explanation for this. This wasn't addressed

11. You notice that the first action doesn't have a completion date

Post-meeting:
After the meeting the chairman asked you what you thought of your first meeting with 'The Only Way Is Up Ltd'. He recognises that the company's meetings are sometimes chaotic. He said this was as a result of the company growing faster than expected.

They didn't have the funds to provide formal meetings and minute taking training for staff when the company started. Now there isn't time to send staff on a formal training course as everyone is needed to cope with the workload.

The Chief Executive thinks it's time for the company to become more professional in the way it handles meetings. He recognises that the company if probably wasting time and money in some instances. He wants to start with this meeting and then roll out new working practices for all company meetings.

Your task:
The Chief Executive knows you are an experienced meeting secretary and minute taker. He would value your feedback on the following:

1. Explain what was wrong with the meeting you attended

2. The chairman would like you to confirm the meeting secretary's role. He wants to share this information with all the staff to help them plan better meetings

3. The chairman would like you to explain where the minute taker takes over from the meeting secretary. He wants to share this information with

all the staff to help make meetings a more efficient use of company time and money

4. All the company's meetings are monthly. Confirm the timescale for issuing the agenda and minutes

5. Create a basic agenda template that can be used for all future company meetings

6 Create a minutes template that can be used for all future company meetings

7. Suggest the style of minutes the company should use for future meetings

8. Suggest how the minute taker could be more effective

9. Create a set of minutes for the three actions from this meeting

The Chief Executive would like you to present your findings in a short report. How you choose to present your report is up to you. He would like a separate document for the actions from this meeting.

The aim of this exercise was to consolidate everything that is covered in 'Success Starts Here'.

I hope this book has provided you with some useful information to help you hone your minute taking skills. Perhaps you have also identified ways to improve the planning and preparation of your meetings.

If you have any comments, observations or questions about minute taking I would be delighted to hear from you. Shepherd Creative Learning welcomes feedback, postive or negative. If you would like to get in touch with us our email address is shepherdcreativelearning@gmail.com.

The final word goes to Dennis Waitley. "The winners in life think constantly in terms of I can, I will, and I am. Losers, on the other hand, concentrate their waking thoughts on what they should have or would have done, or what they can't do". Think like a winner and know you can be a great minute taker!

11. Terms

The terms in this chapter can relate to formal, business and informal meetings.

Absent - These are the people who were expected to attend the meeting. They didn't turn up or send their apologies

Any other business - This is an agenda item for emergency use only. This is an opportunity to discuss urgent matters that came to light after the agenda was issued

Attendees - This can be anyone attending the meeting. This includes the chairperson, minute taker, attendees, visitors or observers

Chairperson - The person running the meeting. This is not necessarily the most senior person in the room

Chairperson's brief - This is also known as the chairperson's agenda. It's simply a more detailed agenda than the version issued to the other attendees

Contributors - These are also referred to as attendees. These can be people who attended all or part of the meeting. As the name suggests they are expected to contribute to the meeting in some way. Anyone who doesn't contribute and isn't there as an observer should leave/not attend in future

Declarations of interest - These are a potential conflict of interest relating to one (or more) of the agenda items. Declarations of interest should be declared at the start of the meeting

In attendance - This term is used for formal meetings only. The term refers to people present, who aren't board members

Matters arising - These are the actions from the previous meeting. Ideally each action should be closed at the current meeting, not carried forward to future meetings

Meeting secretary - The person creating and issuing the agenda and other documents for discussion at the meeting. Note: often the meeting secretary and minute taker are the same person

Minutes of the previous meeting - These are the minutes from the previous meeting. At the current meeting, these minutes will be adopted or amended

Minute taker - The person responsible for taking notes in the meeting and creating and issuing the minutes

Observers - People who have been invited to observe the meeting. Only the chairperson should invite observers. Observers are not permitted to participate in the meeting, but they should be there for a specific reason e.g. future minute taker

Substitutes - These are people who are deputising for a regular member of the group, who is unable to attend. Substitutes are expected to participate in the discussions are far as possible. Otherwise there is no point in them attending the meeting

Visitors - These are people who don't normally attend the meeting. They have usually been invited to deliver a presentation, lead a discussion or contribute to a specific agenda item. Visitors aren't normally expected to stay for the entire meeting

12. Appendices

In this chapter you will find the answers to the exercises earlier in the book.

12.1 Exercise: Quick Minute Taking Quiz - Answers

Here are the answers to the Quick Minute Taking Quiz in chapter 1.

1. Three

2. No. Unless your organisation has a policy on style of minutes, select the style most appropriate for your meeting

3. No. The changes should be saved for the next meeting

4. No. Only those people who attended the meeting are entitled to a copy. Everyone else needs to get the chairperson's permission

5. No. The chairperson is the document owner

6. No. The minute taker should not participate in the discussions. If you are expected to participate in any of the discussions someone else should take the minutes

7. No. The minutes should be issued within five working days of the meeting

12.2 Exercise: Planning the Meeting Quiz - Answers

Here are the answers to the questions in chapter 6.

1. You could be asked to do any or all or the following - book the meeting room, refreshments and parking spaces. You may also be asked to invite the attendees and brief them on what is expected of them, create and issue the agenda and obtain updates regarding all the actions from the previous meeting

2. Basic, full and objectives agenda. The basic agenda is commonly used for business meetings. In theory any style of agenda could be used for any type of meeting

3. Apologies, Welcome, introductions and administration, Minutes of the previous meeting, Matters arising, Reports, Main agenda items, Any other business, Date of next meeting

4. No. Each main agenda item should have its own agenda item number and heading

5. No. 'Apologies' appears at the top of the agenda but is just listed as a reminder for attendees to send their apologies if they know they won't be attending

6. It's good practice for the chairperson to approve the agenda, but if they aren't available or refuse then it will have to be issued without their consent

7. The name of the group or the meeting, date and start time of the meeting, and the meeting venue

8. The primary difference between these two styles of agenda is the terminology used. The objectives agenda provides clear guidance on what has to be achieved rather than what is to be discussed

9. The chairperson's agenda includes timings and details of the desired outcome for each agenda item. It also contains any background information that might be helpful to the chairperson during the meeting

10. The nine tasks are:

1. Read and understand the context of each agenda item

2. Talk to contributors to clarify any points you don't understand

3. Obtain a list of any jargon likely to be used in the meeting

4. Know which style of minutes you will be creating

5. Print a copy of the minutes for signing (if required) and a copy of the minutes for personal reference

6. Print a copy of all documents that form part of the meeting

7. Ensure you have a supply of pens or pencils that you like writing with

8. Prepare the notepad

9. Print spare copies of the agenda, reports and any other documents issued with the agenda

11. No, due to the nature of the meeting

12. To discuss any help or support either party needs during the meeting, agree who will be responsible for time-keeping, agree how contentious or sensitive items will be minuted, confirm any updates for the matters arising and confirm if the chairperson wants a register for signing

12.3 Exercise: Précis the Matters Arising - Answers

Here are the answers to the Précis the Matters Arising exercise in chapter 7. Your choice of wording may be slightly different, but here is the information that should have been captured for the minutes:

Neighbour dispute: This dispute has now been resolved to everyone's satisfaction. This action is completed

Fence falling down: Dinosaurs 'R' Us Housing Group has replaced the fence at 32 Rockhard Road. This action is completed

Broken window: Mr and Mrs Stoneface have been given three weeks to repair the broken window at 19 Boulder Boulevard. If the repair isn't carried out we will do it and add the cost to their rent. This action is in hand

12.4 Exercise: Record the Actions - Answers

Here are the answers to the Create an Actions Document exercise in chapter 7. Your wording may be slightly different, but here is a suggested layout for presenting this information.

4. Promoting Tourism
The actions from this discussion are:

Tivon Quigley will create a draft letter inviting local businesses to participate in promoting tourism in the town. The draft letter will be discussed and approved at the next meeting

Yaffa Auld, Ava Chan and Ziv Singh will compile a list of potential local restaurants and cafés to get involved in a discount voucher scheme. Target date - next meeting

We are going to work with the theatre to promote their special event celebrating International Women's Day. Adeline Galbraith will be the primary point of contact. She will create a press release for the event. Target date - next meeting

Yachne Dabney will obtain some quotes for a new logo. Doron Gwin will draft some new text for our website. Target date - next meeting

12.5 Exercise: To Minute or Not - Answers

Here are the answers to the To Minute or Not exercise in chapter 8. Your choice of wording may be slightly different, but here is the information that should have been captured for the minutes:

Scenario 1:
1. No. The minutes should be a summary of what was discussed, not a record of what was said. You would only make a word-for-word record if it was a disciplinary meeting with the senior member of staff

2. The rules of minute taking are clear - people should never be named in the minutes

3. The minutes should be a summary of the discussion. The minutes should confirm that a motion has been passed to dismiss [name of the senior staff member]. For future reference it might be helpful to confirm why the motion to dismiss has been passed

Scenario 2:
1. No. There are unsubstantiated claims in this document. Minuting this could lead to a grievance from the injured party

2. Do not name the person making the statement. Depending on what is discussed you may need to name the person the statement is about. Check with the chairperson

3. The chairperson is responsible for deciding what should be minuted. Due to the contentious nature of this discussion minute as little information as possible

12.6 Exercise: Create Summary Minutes From Your Notes - Answers

Here are the answers to the Create Summary Minutes From Your Notes exercise in chapter 8. Your wording may be slightly different, but here is a suggested layout for presenting this information.

4. Promoting Tourism
[Summary of the discussion]. The actions from this discussion are:
Create a draft letter inviting local businesses to participate in promoting tourism in the town. The draft letter will be discussed and approved at the next meeting
Tivon Quigley date of next meeting

Compile a list of potential local restaurants and cafés to get involved in a discount voucher scheme
Yaffa Auld, Ava Chan and Ziv Singh date of next meeting

Work with the theatre to promote their special event celebrating International Women's Day Adeline Galbraith will be the primary point of contact. Create a press release for the event

Adeline Galbraith Ethan Schmidt date of next meeting

Obtain some quotes for a new logo. Draft some new text for our website
Yachne Dabney and Doron Gwin date of next meeting

12.7 Exercise: Agenda and Minute Taking Quiz - Answers

Here are the answers to the Agenda and Minute Taking Quiz in chapter 10.

1. Answer - C. It's fine to issue them earlier than this, but they should not be issued any closer to the meeting date than this

2. The three styles of agenda are - basic, full and objectives

3. The style of agenda no longer commonly used is the objectives agenda

4. The chairperson should decide who is going to create the agenda. He/she is the owner of the document even if he/she delegates the task of writing it to someone else

5. For formal meetings the agenda should always be approved before it's issued. This is due to the serious nature of the meeting. For business meetings, ideally yes. The agenda can be issued without the chairperson's approval but this might be problematic during the meeting. In the case of informal meetings; not all informal meetings have an agenda

6. The three categories of meeting are - formal, business and informal

7. The chairperson's agenda is more detailed than the one issued to everyone else. Typically it will contain timings, expected outcomes for each agenda item, background information, and any other information that might be useful during the meeting

8. The person creating the agenda for the meeting; usually creates the chairperson's agenda too. The chairperson should have some input into this document

9. Take as many notes as you feel you need to. You need sufficient notes to enable you to create clear, concise and accurate minutes. Experienced minute takers generally take fewer notes

10. You should include a summary of the action, action owner and a completion date. Without this information you can't hold the action owner accountable

11. If the chairperson doesn't confirm the details of the actions, speak up. Don't allow the meeting to move forward until this information has been agreed and captured

12. The three different styles of minutes are - summary, verbatim and action point

13. Summary minutes are the style most commonly used for business meetings?

14. Answer - B. Although the minute taker is responsible for creating the minutes, the chairperson is the document owner

15. Minutes relating to formal meetings should always be approved. In the case of business meetings and informal meetings it's good practice to do so